THE RULES OF
SOCIOLOGICAL METHOD

THE RULES
OF SOCIOLOGICAL
METHOD

By ÉMILE DURKHEIM

Late Professor in the Faculty of Letters in the University of Paris

EIGHTH EDITION, TRANSLATED BY

SARAH A. SOLOVAY and JOHN H. MUELLER

AND EDITED BY

GEORGE E. G. CATLIN

Sometime Professor of Politics in Cornell University

THE FREE PRESS OF GLENCOE

REPRINTED AUGUST 1950, SEPTEMBER 1958

THIRD PRINTING AUGUST 1962

To

CHARLES AUSTIN BEARD

Humanist

in affectionate respect

—G. E. G. C.

TRANSLATORS' NOTE

The translators desire to express sincere gratitude to Dr. N. C. Leites, graduate student of Cornell University, for his generous aid and suggestions in the work of translation.

TABLE OF CONTENTS

INTRODUCTION TO THE TRANSLATION

I

This is one of the briefest of the works of Émile Durkheim (1858–1917), professor of social science in the University of Bordeaux and, later, professor of sociology and education in the University of Paris, and editor-in-chief of *L'Année sociologique*. It is also one of the most important of his works.

There are few sociological writers—not only in France— of more significance than M. Durkheim. His study on suicide (1897) can be fitly placed along with the works of Charles Booth, Flexner, and W. I. Thomas and with like endeavors to study the social structure, the disturbances from which the body politic suffers, and the factors determinant of these perturbations. His *Division du travail social* (1893) has largely shaped the solidarist school of political philosophy and left a profound mark upon the theory of law expounded by such authorities as the late Professor Léon Duguit. In it Durkheim, like Marx, developed ideas earlier traced by Adam Smith. *Les Règles de la méthode sociologique* (1895) is a treatise which raises most of those theoretical problems which are fundamental to a study of human organization. It is a classic in sociology and in the methodology of political science. It constitutes an admirable introduction to these subjects, no less by the warnings which the weaknesses of this magistral statement should signal to the student than by the soundness of its general design.

Durkheim's work, in common with that of Pareto and many other sociologists, too frequently lacks distinction of manner and lucidity of style. It sometimes fails to avoid labored platitudes. It must, however, be borne in mind that the advancement of science depends, in its initial stages, upon the exact statement even of the commonplace. It is Durkheim's merit that, in this volume, he states his position with brevity and care and avoids that pretentious and often tautological generalization which characterizes the work of Comte and Spencer. Whereas Comte's work substantially does not advance beyond a prophecy of a messianic positivist age, and hence gives countenance to philosophies of history even of the occultist type of Dr. Spengler's, Durkheim endeavors to provide a useful delimitation of the phenomena which students of the groundwork of human organization are called upon to study and a modest method by which this material may be treated fruitfully.

It does not detract from our debt to him, for this manual in method, that some of his sociological theories (not always the most fortunate) were anticipated or influenced by Wundt, Espinas (1878), Tönnies (1887), and Simmel (1890). Durkheim, neither in the volume here translated nor elsewhere, attempts to establish or elaborate a new science. His interest is not in some sociological science but in a sociological method utilizing a certain distinctive approach and supposition. His object is to provide a new instrument to be used by all social sciences, such as economics and (presumably) political science, and by disciplines which he laxly calls sciences, such as the studies of the history of religion and of art.

In connection with his suggested method Professor Durkheim raises in this book two issues, cardinal in importance for all sciences directly concerned with human relationships, whether economic, political, or genetic. For this reason this short pamphlet is still not only a landmark in the history of

the social sciences but a beacon burning as a guide to travel-
ing students. These issues lie in (1) the discussion of the
possibility of social sciences, strictly so called, as distinct
from such sciences as zoölogy, on the one hand, and psychology, on the other; and (2) the more specific discussion of the
existence, in social phenomena, of mensurable forces or
"facts"—objective, resistant, and persistent—in relation to
the will of the individual, such as might constitute part of
the data of economic science and all the data of political
science.

Durkheim rightly insists (a) that there is a genuine distinction of field or plane between the natural and the social
sciences, and (b) that the methods of science applicable in
the field of the natural sciences are, nevertheless, valid within the social field. On the other hand, attempts are common
to absorb the social sciences into the province of an enlarged
psychology. Against this, Durkheim (c) well points out that
social phenomena, far from being the product of the individual's own ideas or will, opinion or caprice, or even of the
mere wish of his fellows, have a constraining influence upon
the individual and even upon the aggregate of these individuals.

In his discussion of the significance of the volume and
density of population (which is assuredly not a matter of
individual psychology or even, directly, of the operation of
the "social mind") Durkheim emphasizes the part played
by two of those constraining material factors that mould the
data of politics and economics and are the very objects of
study of genetics. This constraining power inheres not in
the psychological qualities alone of the situation but in the
fact of society itself and of the necessary cohabitation, under
material and economic conditions, of a multiplicity of indi-

viduals with biological, as well as psychological, needs—a "multiple-individual situation."

What Durkheim does not accurately apprehend is the nature of this constraint which, cutting the Gordian knot of patient study, he attributes to the operation, upon a higher plane of experience, of some collective consciousness. This very hypothetical entity he tends to posit as his major "social fact." It is, moreover, itself a composite of psycho-social facts. However, in the course of this discussion he is necessarily led to undertake.the important task of giving precision to the use of this term "social fact" in a technical sense as involving constants and permanents. The task is important since the issue of the very existence of social sciences, properly so called, depends upon whether their data have such objectivity and persistency as to permit the generalizations, founded on one set of observations, to be verified on all subsequent occasions, under like conditions, by any intelligent and impartial observer using the appropriate method.

Durkheim's method, most suggestive in itself, yet involves, it so happens, the use of the hypothesis of a collective consciousness; it results in a deplorable effort to interpret social phenomena in terms of this alleged consciousness. In this Durkheim is at one with a series of writers—theorists of the "social organism"—excellently discussed by Professor Coker of Yale. Durkheim, however, is not singular among men of science in being more valuable in respect of the by-products of his theory than in his main contention.

II

What Durkheim means by "social facts" is clearly only to be understood by reference to the context of his discussion. He does not mean any facts having to do with society, as understood in common parlance. In a given experience, such as an orchestral concert, there is one set of facts, or objective events, of which the physicist takes cognizance and another set which alone has meaning for the musical critic. M. Durkheim lays down, as he is fully entitled to do, two empirical tests of the existence of a "social fact." The first of these is that it has the property of "being general throughout the extent of a given society" (p. 13), at a given stage in the evolution of that society. Durkheim here, by implication, distinguishes a social fact from a psychological fact which is universal to human nature. Moreover, he does not here mean that the fact is existent without exception—e.g., that all men are suicides or drunkards—but that it is potentially universal in the sense that, granted given conditions, it will anywhere be set up. Its incidence is general.

The second test that he applies is that a social fact is marked by "any manner of action, whether of a set nature or otherwise, capable of exercising over the individual exterior constraint" (p. 13). Elsewhere he states, more precisely, "A social fact is to be recognized by the coercive power which it exercises or is capable of exercising over individuals; and the presence of this power is, in turn, to be recognized by the existence of some determinate sanction or by the resistance which this fact opposes to every endeavor which tends to do violence to it" (p. 10).

In a brief study of Durkheim's method by M. Roger Lacombe, the point is well made that Durkheim uses his second test as additional to the first, rather than as a limit upon it. Thus the empirical constants in the phenomena of suicide and of the marriage- and death-rates Durkheim treats as "social facts" on the ground that they are, as

Buckle saw, permanencies of social life apparently only subject to slight and slow variations, although they are not
themselves compulsive or constraining forces. At times, indeed, it is true that Durkheim seems dangerously near
personifying them and, by this animism, to endowing them
with force. However, these facts are distinguishable alike
from those laws and traditions that authorize physical or
moral pressure on the individual and from those manners
and customs, such as the use of a language, not reinforced
by any specific social sanction, which yet doom to practical
failure individual enterprises that have the rashness to ignore or flout them.

Precision and consistency can only be introduced into
Durkheim's "tests" (he elsewhere unfortunately disclaims
any intention of supplying a logical "definition") if stress be
laid upon the notion of the resistance by social structures
to the individual will and of the pressure by this structure
in controlling the activities of individuals. Under such a use
of terms any particular suicide or the aggregate of suicides
would not be, technically, a "social fact," as distinct from
any other historical incident; but the student of suicide
might well discover that the constant fact of the suicide
rate was a "social fact," as exercising a permanent influence
on the custom of the rest of the population. It might set up
or perpetuate particular precautions or checks. He might
discover that it was due to the interplay of such permanent
psychological factors as a morbid egoism and of the opera-
tive "social facts" of religious checks and of traditional domestic influences. Similarly, such a historical incident as frequency of drunkenness becomes a "social fact" when it can
be shown to be a permanent factor involuntarily affecting
the life of the rest of the population, which social fact itself

may possibly be analyzable into terms of sense of inferiority, influence of poverty, and the like.[1] If there are physical and demographical permanencies or constant processes and there are psychological permanents, we are entitled to presume social permanents where these fields interlock.

Since, in popular phraseology, any result whatsoever of a social situation, such as the casual conversation of people in a room, is a social fact, the technical use of this term has its embarrassments and requires precision. In some, but not all, cases the term "social structure" would better cover the meaning. Further, the customary use of the term "social fact," with reference to highly organic situations, may well tend to that bane of the social sciences, the confusion of organic and "rich" situations, that are impermanent, with the elementary but more humble ones such as must be the first objects of scientific study. Such elements as the power relationship of individual wills tend to be overlooked, while attention is concentrated upon impressive historical structures such as the state. Political science is not, in this fashion, advanced. These criticisms, however, do not seem to have such weight as to give a reason for rejecting the technical use of Durkheim's term.

One initial problem, however, is not yet solved. These "social facts" of Durkheim, the constants in the suicide- and marriage-rate, or in drunkenness and crime, or even that increasing interdependence of the members of society which he expounded in his great book *De la division du travail social*, and the psychological facts (objective to the actor) of a given culture, are not absolute permanencies such as the formula for carbon monoxide. They are merely very per-

[1] See George E. G. Catlin, *Liquor Control* ("Home University Library") (New York, 1931), pp. 231 ff.

sistent historical phenomena which it merely obscures scientific intelligence to suppose to be unchangeable. Let us say frankly that the instances of "social facts" cited by Durkheim are instances containing a large element of the contingent.

There are, however, we may properly assert, some absolute permanencies within the field of reference, some elemental social acts. Such permanencies are the psychological demand for freedom; the nonpsychological fact of population with its corollaries, the facts of social relationship, of the wills of others, of the conditioning of these wills by death and birth; the nonpsychological facts of food and clothing and the attendant conditions which compel economic activity under varying limits always set by geography, technology, local culture, and so forth. These facts, compounded in their simplest relations, become social facts of an entirely permanent nature.

"Two men purposing something and their wills conditioned each by the action of the other" is an instance of a social situation of the most universal nature. It is obviously not "a law." The formulation of the rules of conditioned action, if constant, would be a law, e.g., if we could conclude (rather as James Mill did conclude), that "if either would act freely, he *must* acquire authority over the other." The exercise of this authority, in such a situation, might merit being called an elementary "social fact."

Needless to say, as in every other field—astronomy, biology, hydraulics, optics—richness is given to the study by the introduction of the contingent, whether it be the contingencies of "natural history" or of human history. It is enough that there is some rock of permanency—some situation, in brief, in which the hypothetical conditions and axiomata of science are readily and steadily fulfilled—upon which principles of interpretation may rest. The analysis provided by Durkheim appears to be of high significance in detecting the essentials of sound method but to be defective in precision.

III

A reason may be discovered for this defect. Durkheim imagined that he had discovered certain central principles which saved the trouble of more meticulous research. His "social facts" have an unsatisfactory complexity and a vasty air to them. These principles are peculiarly displayed in connection with his studies on primitive religion and are, indeed, no less superstitious than the beliefs which he flatters himself that he explains. Here again Durkheim's failings establish a series of warnings for students which they neglect to study at their peril. The first of these weaknesses is similar to that of most of the exponents of a so-called "science of history"; the second relates to his supposition of a "collective consciousness"; the third is connected with his confusion—in which he was followed by his eminent disciple, M. Léon Duguit—between science and ethics.

As touching the first point, on the basis of particular studies Durkheim appears to commit himself to the very dubious proposition that the course of cultural evolution, for some occult reason, is the same in all countries, and that the only matter of difference is that of the stage of evolution reached, or, at least, that in history, as a whole, a clearly marked course is to be descried. Upon some such premise of historical determinism, cognized and mapped, most of the pseudo-sciences of history are built. It is forgotten that history is, by its nature, nominalistic—peculiarly a knowledge of the particular, waiting for insight to bring its bones together. The argument rests upon a confusion between the correct statement that certain logical deductions infallibly follow from certain hypotheses (and that these basic hypotheses concerning social constants are, in some cases, fulfilled with sufficient frequency for deductions about consequences to be verifiable) and the entirely different proposition that certain historical events do inevitably occur or repeat themselves, thanks to some immanent logic.

Durkheim is not content to say—as, for example, Pareto said, and as is now a generally accepted hypothesis among significant students professionally acquainted with the field —that a common method is utilizable in the natural and social sciences. He requires more than this statement, as an instrument of exploration, and desires some short cut to scientific results.

Much argument has been directed toward a demonstration that the methods of the natural sciences, which involve the use of types and the grounding of generalizations upon typical action, are inapplicable in the human field where that which is most significant is individual and particular. This consideration is indeed fatal to any claims on behalf of any so-called "science of culture," or "science of history" unless the word "science" is to be used vaguely, as merely equivalent to "knowledge," and is to become in effect synonymous with a philosophy or evaluation.

Although the German word *Wissenschaft* has sometimes a broader connotation, the word "science" is generally and suitably used in English to imply systematic knowledge of which the conclusions or generalizations can be verified by any impartial observer using an appropriate method. Frequently, although not necessarily, this systematic knowledge is regarded as carrying with it the implication of power or control. Conclusions reached concerning the value of cultures admit of no such generalizations as can be verified by a method independent of subjective opinion—unless we assume, with Windelband and Rickert, that it is demonstrable that certain values are both absolutely valid and are apprehensible as such.[2]

It may readily be conceded that no political science, i.e., no science of the social organization of wills, is likely greatly to deepen our appreciation of the works of Shakespeare and Racine or of the Renaissance in Florence. I leave it to Marxists to discuss whether economic interpretation can do this. Since, however, political science and sociology are not, I suggest, the study of "collective mental activity" or of cultural reality or of cultural evolution (which are the concerns of psychology, philosophy, and history), such an admission is not damaging. Whether "social psychology," in any sense other than an individual psychology bearing upon social situations, can make any reply to this challenge is perhaps more questionable. Eminent psychologists are probably justified who decline to see any significance whatsoever in the term "social psychology," save as the psychological study of the individual in a social context or as a pretense for introducing mysticism into an alien sphere.

Politics, it may be suggested, and its propaedeutic study, sociology, are concerned with exactly the same kind of abstract deduction from certain hypotheses, generally corresponding with observed psychological and social occurrences, as that with which economics is concerned. They present no greater and no smaller methodological difficulties

[2] I take it that this is the position favored by Professor Dennes in his able study on *The Method and Presuppositions of Group Psychology* (Berkeley, Calif., 1924).

than that science. Their humble business will be to understand that which is common to human behavior in frequently recurring social situations, and not with that which is valuable because distinctive, if not unique. It is philosophy and poetry alone that are concerned with the "essential stuff and character of real societies" or with the "spiritual characters of social groups." Equally, the politicist is not concerned with "all manifestations of human society" but with certain very limited manifestations, deliberately abstracted for study so as to yield to treatment by a satisfactory methodological process.

The simplest social acts do, indeed, repeat themselves with such frequency that we may legitimately take them as the foundations of some economic or political science, making the reasonable hypothesis that they will continue to repeat themselves. If, on the other hand, there are uniformities in the gross masses of social phenomena—e.g., in national cultures—these uniformities are not proved by science but are the data for some science as yet undeveloped. For the rest, the existence, beyond coincidence, of such repetitions in any large-scale fashion, or of "grand cycles," must be held to be vehemently suspect. This is not, of course, to say that psychological, economic, and political causes, when they happen to arise in forms in effect identical, do not produce results in effect identical. The indication of such identities is the task of the social sciences. The forecast, however, that certain results must occur in such or such a country or century is the work of our modern astrologers and is worth about as much as the old astrology. It rests upon an intuition not granted to reason.

In the case of Durkheim, however, his prejudice in favor of regarding social facts as the manifestation of the will or purpose of some occult collective mind, rather than any elaborated philosophy of history, predisposes him to start his studies (although he is too good a student of his field to let this supposition interfere with him unduly in his actual researches) from the thesis of the influence of complicated social forces, which are manifestations of this mind, rather than from the simplest available data.

IV

The theory of a social mind or collective consciousness—Durkheim rejects the phrase "social soul," since he also denies the existence of an individual soul—has a long and unhappy history, ever since the days when Plato, the Church Fathers, and (illogically enough) Hobbes found, in the notion of a conscious body politic, a convenient metaphor. The rapid advance of biology in the nineteenth century, like the advance of mathematics in the sixteenth century, set fashions in thought. Organic analogies were in the air, and the development of psychology enabled these analogies to be used without any obligation on the part of theorists to tie themselves down to the precision of gross physical details. It encouraged this baneful use of metaphors in a fashion which suggested philosophical profundity by confounding the doctrine of a group mind with the older theory of the state as a moral entelechy or as a legal entity. Durkheim refers to his doctrine as, not materialistic, but as "hyper-spiritual."

In his article on "Représentations individuelles et représentations collectives" (1898) he maintains that any attempt to resolve the collective consciousness into the interrelation of individual consciousnesses is open to the same objection as a materialist attempt to resolve individual consciousness into a mere interrelation of nerve cells of the brain.[3] That, by his own argument, these cells and the individual consciousness belong to sharply different orders of existence, whereas individual and collective consciousnesses do not, is an objection to which Durkheim gives no attention proportionate to the importance of the role which an emergent collective consciousness plays in his works.

In dealing with this knotty point, it is essential to bear in mind the pluralistic nature of Durkheim's concept of the individual mind. This theory of *représentations collectives* (see pp. 102 ff.) does not *necessarily* lead over to the same practical consequences as the monistic theory of a group-mind or even of a constellation of national group-minds. A scholastic defense of Durkheim can indicate that his theory is patent of an interpretation even neorealist in its implications. Certainly Durkheim assimilated the collective and the individual consciousness by pluralizing the latter. The social mind is equally a composite. Moreover, the social theory of many of Durkheim's disciples is bereft of "group-mind" dogmatism; and Durkheim himself may be acquitted of any graver charge than lack of caution. Nevertheless, the issue is a cardinal one. He has the solid excuse that here, as in his concrete sociological studies, he is endeavoring to correct, by stress on social milieu, the unwarrantable individualism and atomism of Spencer's *political* theory and, still more, of the contemporary economists. "The *représentations collectives* are the highest form of psychic life, since they are the

---

[3] See on this point the acute criticism by S. Deploige, *Le Conflit de la morale et de la sociologie* (1927); also Morris Ginsburg, *The Psychology of Society*, and C. E. Gehlke, *Émile Durkheim's Contributions to Sociological Theory*. A distinctive theory of Durkheim's doctrine of consciousness is ably maintained by Professor Talcott Parsons in a work of which the publication is eagerly expected.

representation of representations," writes Durkheim. And again society—each society—is "the highest reality of the intellectual and moral order." Such phrases, redolent with valuations, are, to put it leniently, ambiguous, where the charge is one of dogmatizing ahead of all knowledge and of making a dust that blinds the eyes of sociological science. Even genius, which may explain all, does not excuse all.

The *représentation collective* corresponds in the psychological order, as M. Marcel Mauss, M. Durkheim's nephew, points out, to the notion of the totality of the society.[4] It involves the notion of common social descent, tradition, "myth," and has intimate relations with the origins of authority and discipline. Hence the practical difference between a social consciousness no less plural than the individual ones of Jones or Smith, ordering me to obey, and a group consciousness just as personal as those of Jones or Smith, requiring my obedience, wears somewhat thin. Durkheim, in advancing from a simple theory of collective consciousness to the elaborated one of "collective re-presentations," took over a doctrine to be found in Renouvier which was later accepted, significantly enough, by M. Bergson. The political implications of Durkheim's solidarist theory were adequately shown later.

[4] On this vexed issue the actual words of M. Mauss (*L'Année sociologique*, nouvelle série, II, 126) merit attention: "Il faudrait encore considérer le tout de celles-ci (représentations collectives), la conscience collective. De même que psychologiquement, l'homme pense, se tend, agit, sent à la fois, avec tout son corps, de même cette communauté des corps et des esprits qu'est une société sent, agit, vit et *veut vivre* avec tous les corps et avec tous les esprits de tous ces hommes. Elle est leur tout, le tout de ces touts; elle est cela et rien d'autre; ce qui est assez. ... C'est ainsi qu'on pourra,—peut-être en faisant appel à d'autres sciences, biologiques en particulier, plutôt que psychologiques,—arriver à *une science du corps et de l'âme des sociétés*. De ce point de vue, le problème complet de la conscience collective et de la raison pourront peut-être être abordés objectivement." (*Italics mine.*)

The repeated acceptance of variants of the group-consciousness theory, in view of the weakness of most of the arguments adduced in its favor, can perhaps be explained only on the supposition that wish is here the parent of thought. In the case of such writers as Stahl (1802–61) the advantage is plain to patriotism and to the moral authority of the state, as an ethical object of devotion, could that state be endowed with a personality more than legal. In the case of Durkheim, while there is a reaction against the romantic idealism of the school of Cousin, with its abstract dogmas, there is an uneasy desire to escape the accusation of "materialism" and to save morality. It is hoped that a positivist ethics may do the trick. Durkheim (himself of rabbinical parentage) wishes to provide French anticlericals with as good a moral authority as that upheld by the Catholic church, with its appeal to a scholastic rationalism based on revelation. The theory reaches its appropriate completion in Durkheim's patriotic articles during the last war.

As Durkheim says, "We have decided to give our children a purely lay education."[5] It is therefore convenient if society can take on godlike attributes; and in his *Elementary Forms of Religious Life* (Paris, 1912) Durkheim had already reached the conclusion that the notion of God and his authority are a sublimation of the clan, regarded as a collectivity, and of its social authority. The elegance of the solution of the problem, if this collectivity can be found to have a "mind" of its own, as distinct from the existence of a mere prosaic "public opinion" of an interrelated society of human beings, is patent. The more modest and warrantable doctrine according to which a new and emergent level of common experience can be detected in the complicated life of

---

[5] *L'Éducation morale* (Paris, 1925), p. 3. These lectures were published posthumously; Durkheim died on November 15, 1917.

modern human societies (as distinct from the type of experience of the individual in the primitive society of the early family), and according to which a public opinion can be found hardening into a wider social tradition, has no such theological strength. It is perhaps noteworthy that the evolutionary assumptions of those psychologists and anthropologists of whom, e.g., M. Gerald Heard provides a popular and suggestive interpretation are the precise contrary.

Further, granted the existence of a collective consciousness, the problem is also solved for Durkheim of what is the specific subject matter of the vagrant science of sociology. It is merely necessary to limit psychology by definition to the level of individual consciousness and a virgin field is left ready for the tilling. The sole disadvantage of this procedure is that the interesting and astonishing conclusion that there is a collective consciousness, which should be reached at the end of the scientific study, is hastily postulated at the beginning of it. It must, however, be pointed out in defense of Durkheim that most of his life-work lay along lines which necessarily led to preoccupation with the compulsive effects upon the individual of customs which certainly did not seem to be imposed by "reason," regarded in the intellectual or *cérébral* fashion best appreciated by the nineteenth century. Moreover, Durkheim was not only under the influence of Schaeffle (1831–1903) and Wundt (1832–1920) but also of Espinas, who, in his studies on animal society, had called attention to precisely those phases of hive life which, by displaying the power of instinct upon a co-operating mass of insects, presents the greatest difficulties to an individualist and, still more, to an intellectualist explanation. Durkheim does not escape, despite all his verbal claims to be a rationalist.

The association of disbelief in reason in the intellectual

field with belief in the state-leviathan, as the most obvious incarnation of a superhuman social consciousness, in the political field, is an outstanding mark of our present-day culture in this epoch of retrogression. Although (as Professor Sorokin well points out) Durkheim's commentator, Dr. Gehlke, perhaps too closely associates the separate doctrines of Bergson and Durkheim, it is yet true that Bergson and Durkheim, with Schaeffle, alike contribute to the creation of an intellectual climate in which Sorel grew—Georges Sorel, of whom Mussolini has written, "Were it not for Sorel, I should not be what I am." By his ill-considered and scientifically pretentious psycho-mysticism Durkheim has contributed to give the color of justification to the new religion of the altar of *divus Augustus* and to the neopagan philosophy of Caesar-worship. This (scholastically speaking) "realistic" attitude toward society, although applied by Durkheim in sociology,[6] as by Gierke in jurisprudence, for the benefit of the group, was philosophically indispensable for the new religion of the state. Political monism reappeared, out of the political pluralism in vogue in the first quarter of this century, in a form more formidable than even Hobbes ever dreamed.

V

Durkheim's third difficulty is one radical to the whole distinction between a political science, or any other social science such as economics, and a political philosophy.

His division between the social and the psychological field is of an entirely artificial nature, owing to his arbitrary limitation of psychology. His stress is upon the objectivity to the

[6] Cf. the preface to the second edition of the *Division du travail social* (Macmillan Co.), translated by my friend and former student, Dr. George Simpson. Especial attention is called to p. xxvii of Dr. Simpson's introduction.

individual of social phenomena; but the material of which he treats is the same as that which is constituent of the "cultural reality" of such a writer as Znaniecki. The stress with Professor Znaniecki is upon the fashion in which the objective material facts, the ritual of religion, the codes of the lawyers, and the like possess significance in view of the particular subjective interpretation which the members of a given society put upon them. This field of data Durkheim proposes to treat by what he calls "the sociological method"; Znaniecki in his later work brings much of it within the field of social psychology. To none of this can exception be taken.

Znaniecki, however, at this point endeavors (following Max Weber and German schools, to which reference has been made) to divide between what he terms the "humanistic sciences," which deal with the phenomena of consciousness and purpose, and the natural sciences. As a consequence he is compelled to introduce a dichotomy into psychology, between physiological psychology and some humanistic science also named "psychology." Durkheim is already provided with a basis of distinction between individual psychology and the study of the activities of his postulated social consciousness, psychic but objective to the actor. A "humanistic science" must, from the nature of the case, regard its function as incompletely performed unless it conclude by providing normative principles. Unfortunately, Durkheim feels under an obligation to do the same and to cross the bridge from the *is* to the *ought*.

Durkheim, despite all his protests, which Duguit echoes, that he is concerned only with facts, explicitly states that his object is to be able to deduce from his studies such norms, and to establish "a science of morality." The positivist obsession takes charge, which denies the distinction of science and ethics, logic based on anthropological fact and values conditioning judgments. Durkheim has the advantage, against more modest writers, of believing that he is studying a supermind, immanent in society, which is possessed of superior moral authority. Unlike Freud, he does not make this god a projection of the individual consciousness or nature.

Fundamentally, for Durkheim, morality reposes upon one value—success. This success or utility, however, has no satisfactory concrete test, since it is not that of the mortal and limited individual but of the immortal and unlimited entity called "society" (or—it is an important variant—"a society)." Here, in collectivity, is the source of authority and of that discipline, exercised through the coercive customs and habits of the community, for which Durkheim, in his *L'Éducation morale*, inculcates respect. "Discipline," writes Durkheim, "has its justification in itself. It is good that man should be disciplined." In fact, however, the nature of the discipline is not entirely indifferent. The customary morals of the tribe are to be revered because they are part of those cohesive forces which enable this totalitarian society to achieve its own survival, immortality, and success. The concepts of duty and of the good find a common support, which binds them together, in society. "Because society" ("a society?") "is above us, it commands us; and, on the other hand, because, while superior to us, it penetrates us and makes part of ourselves, it draws us with that special inspiration that moral ends have for us." It is necessary to awake faith in a common ideal, and "a spiritualised patriotism can furnish this necessary objective." In the case of his follower, Professor Lévy-Bruhl, the intention of passing beyond the confines of a scientific study of social constants (Pareto's "quest for social uniformities, social laws") to lay the foundation of a science of morals is even more consistent and explicit.

Charmont has excellently criticized Duguit for his obvious vacillations between the scientific study of the actual and the normative statement of the ideal. The same criticism applies to his teacher, Durkheim. It may be, as Professor Laski observed in a review of M. Rueff's *From the Physical to the Social Sciences*, that the endeavor to illuminate the field of political science by the methods of objective and experimental study used in the physical sciences (and economics, etc.) is a "great illusion." Laski's position is at least arguable, if probably reactionary. There is, however, nothing to be said for Durkheim's attempt to have the best of both worlds and to survey the realm of values with a tape measure.

Durkheim's expectation appears to be that a study of anthropology will yield principles that can indicate the roads along which human harmony or happiness can and *ought to be* attained. Individual action "solidary" with that of some society alone *can* be successful and alone *ought* to be successful. "The ought" = "the socially successful."

This conclusion appears to be entirely illicit. At the worst, we are back again in a fatalistic "science of history," which, by denying moral choice, eviscerates ethics of meaning. Such an undertaking is founded upon the fallacy that science is unconditioned prophecy. It may, indeed, be a fact that history is determined; but the only science possible is the study of the psychological and sociological forces constantly at work, and not some astrologer's almanac of future events. At best, we are endeavoring to establish a systematic and verifiable "science of what ought to be."

No science, however, founded on observation, can dictate to us human norms and purposes. Our value judgment of right may well be in defiance of all customs that anthropology may display to us from its storehouse of curious lore and upon which it generalizes. The criticism by Deploige here appears to be final. Only two bases of a science of ethics would appear to be possible. Of these, the first would involve the affirmation, with Spinoza and the Cambridge Platonists, that moral norms for the rational conscience can be deduced by strict logic from certain axioms so as to form a closed, self-consistent, and irrefragable ethical system. Such a thesis involves the existence of self-evident or revealed moral truths or of necessary moral intuitions. In the alternative, it can be urged that human values are conditioned by the human organism that accepts these values and by the environment that, in turn, conditions this organism. Our attention is rightly directed to psychology, medicine, economics. But the resulting science or agglomerate of social sciences is not ethics, as the study and analysis of values, but a study of the exterior conditions that affect the range, growth, and stress of our values and place limits upon them and their achievement.

It may be that the former study is insignificant without the latter, although one would hesitate to say that a study of music and composition was insignificant without an exact knowledge of sound waves. At least the studies are distinct, and the thesis that there is a science of ethics unproved. Nevertheless, the significance is apparent of the study of the sciences of human life, of the material environment, and of the interrelations, economic and social, of life and environment in human conduct. It is against this environmental background that all confident talk of values must be placed, since all proof of any particular value lies in its power to contribute to the system of other reputed values, and the limiting conditions of this power or efficiency are to be found in the nature and set circumstances of the human instrument.

Durkheim's work, more sane than the closed logic of Hegel, upon the one hand, or than the monistic materialism of Marx, upon the other, may serve to call attention to this dependence of the values of the individual upon the laws governing all human nature. It may contribute to a renewed interest in "natural law," as a limiting formula—but this time, to an objective natural law. By this is meant a natural law formulated from patient observation and not—setting aside the contradiction of a "subjective natural law"—a natural law resting on theological certitudes, although recognizant of supports in instinct and reason.

VI

The field of the social sciences lies where the conscious mind is in a particular kind of relationship—a relationship with objects other than itself which exercise upon it constraint, whether with a number of conscious individuals or with "things" or activities, such as the economic, involving a mixed relationship of minds and things. A psychological relationship with something not purely psychological is distinctive of the data of all social sciences.

This "something not purely psychological" which goes to the building-up of the other side of the social relationship and, more permanently, of the social structure, gives peculiar qualities of rigidity to this social structure. It is clear that anything that is "unnatural" from the point of view of human physiology or biology, in the sense that it leads to disorder or decadence, cannot be successfully embodied in it. Objective conditions related to population and raw materials determine this structure and the practicable human relationships within it. The psychological side of the social relationship is by no means entirely plastic, and an increasing knowledge of psychology is likely to give content to the principle that nothing which does violence to the deeper impulses of human nature can expect to be permanent in the conventions or institutions of the social structure. Until that increasing knowledge comes, we live in the dark ages of the politicians and the witch-doctors. These impulses form traditions; and, as Durkheim rightly insists, these traditions are social facts as much as any physiological facts. Traditions, however, are not simply conventionalized impulses. Political traditions represent a compromise between such impulses, the objective fact of social relationship and the needs dictated, and facilities for satisfaction provided, at a given stage of civilization. Economic traditions are similarly dependent upon the conditions of co-operation and of industrial technique, although tradition has, in economics, significance only in terms of the human co-operation and enterprise and not on the purely material side of the relation. Gold and coal have no traditions: only financiers and coal-owners. These constraining facts of conventions and institutions Durkheim excellently insists have significance in fields far broader than the narrow one of civil laws; they operate in fields of religion and industry and wherever the relations of men are subject to obedience to control and rules.

The reader of this little treatise will have it impressed upon him that the world of human society is not something arbitrary and capricious, plastic in the hands of some man of strong will or of some reforming government or of the sovereign people or even of the plain elector. Nor is it merely resistant to arbitrary change with the toughness of what Bagehot called a "cake of custom." This custom represents a *modus vivendi*, slowly discovered, by which man is able to accommodate his physical, psychological, and economic needs in a fashion consistent with some measure of accommodation with his neighbors. This balance has been effected in a fashion consistent with those fundamental laws which are the formulations of the constants of human nature and which govern human conduct. It is a balance supported by the pressure of all those persons who are interested in its maintenance against any intruding and adverse individual or group. Whether this tradition is ethically false and empty or ethically good, so long as the tradition remains this pressure will, in some measure, be applied. The study of these pressures is no small part of political science, which is the formal study of power.

It is the chief merit of Durkheim, as of Lévy-Bruhl, to have called attention to the need for this study. Primarily, Durkheim is a master of method, and of method that achieved results. That is why this present treatise is of such classical importance. Compared with his significance here, Durkheim's "collective-consciousness" heresies are of minor importance. He showed the technique of the study of man in his milieu. Moreover, whether he realized it (as did Duguit) or not, the consequence of his doctrine is, further, to direct attention to the limitations in human nature and in the mechanics of social organization upon any will pretending to sovereign authority above natural law.

If, with one hand, Durkheim as sociologist has built the

structure of popular dictatorship, with the other he has indicated to us the deeper volcanic forces that must destroy
in time, by a certain law of human seismology, every tyran-
ny that does violence to our substantial natures.

GEORGE E. G. CATLIN

AUTHOR'S PREFACE TO THE
FIRST EDITION

We are so little accustomed to treat social phenomena scientifically that certain of the propositions contained in this book may well surprise the reader. However, if there is to be a social science, we shall expect it not merely to paraphrase the traditional prejudices of the common man but to give us a new and different view of them; for the aim of all science is to make discoveries, and every discovery more or less disturbs accepted ideas. Unless, then, sociology attributes to common sense an authority which it has not enjoyed for a long time in other sciences—and it is impossible to see how such authority could be justified—the scholar must resolutely resist being intimidated by the results to which his researches lead, demanding only that they be conducted scientifically. As it is characteristic of the sophist to invite paradoxes, likewise it is a sign of intellectual cowardliness to avoid them when they are imposed on us by the facts.

Unfortunately, it is easier to admit this rule in principle than to apply it consistently in practice. The impulses of common sense are so deeply ingrained in us that it is difficult to eradicate them from sociological discussion. When we consciously free our thoughts of them, they still mold our unconscious judgments; and against such error we have no defense. Only long and special training can teach us to avoid it. The reader must bear in mind that the ways of thinking to which he is most inclined are adverse, rather than favorable, to the scientific study of social phenomena; and he must consequently be on his guard against his first impressions. If he indulges in such loose habits of thought, he is likely to judge this book without having understood it. For example, we might possibly be accused of wishing to condone crime, because we designate it a normal phenomenon. Such a criticism, however, would be quite naïve; for if it is normal that crimes exist in every society, it is equally normal that there be punishment for them. The existence of a repressive system is not less universal than the existence of criminality, nor less indispensable to the collective well-being. A society without criminality would necessitate a standardization of the moral conceptions of all individuals which is neither possible nor desirable, for reasons which will be found below. On the other hand, if there were no system of repression, a certain moral heterogeneity would exist which is irreconcilable with the very existence of society. Common sense, assuming that crime is repugnant to us, wrongly concludes that it could not disappear too completely. With its customary naïveté, it cannot conceive that a thing which is repulsive may still have some usefulness. Yet there is no contradiction in this. Are there not distasteful functions in the physical organism whose regular exercise is necessary for individual health? Do we not dislike suffering? Yet an individual who did not experience it would be abnormal. The normality of a thing, and the sentiments of aversion it inspires, may even be essentially integrated. If pain is normal, it is equally normal that it be disliked; if crime is normal, it is nonetheless undesirable.[1] Our reasoning is not at all revo-

[1] The objection may be raised that if health includes undesirable elements, how can we postulate it, as we do below, as the immediate objective of conduct? We see no contradiction in this. It constantly happens that a thing which is harmful in certain of its consequences is, in others, useful or even necessary to life. If its bad effects are regularly neutralized by an

lutionary. We are even, in a sense, essentially conservative, since we deal with social facts as such, recognize their flexibility, but conceive them as deterministic rather than arbitrary. How much more dangerous is the doctrine which sees in social phenomena only the results of unrestrained manipulation, which can in an instant, by a simple dialectical artifice, be completely upset!

Since it has been customary to think of social life as the logical development of ideal concepts, a method which makes social evolution depend on objective conditions defined in space will perhaps be judged crude and will possibly be termed "materialistic." Yet we could more justly claim the contrary designation. Is not the essence of idealism contained in the idea that psychological phenomena cannot be immediately derived from organic phenomena? Our method is in part only an application of this principle to social facts. Just as the idealists separate the psychological from the biological realm, so we separate the psychological from the social; like them, we refuse to explain the complex in terms of the simple. However, neither of the foregoing appellations is exactly appropriate, and the only designation we can accept is that of "rationalist." As a matter of fact, our principal objective is to extend scientific rationalism to human behavior. It can be shown that behavior of the past, when analyzed, can be reduced to relationships of cause and

---

opposing effect, it is ultimately beneficial. And yet it will always be odious, for it is a constant threat, always needing to be neutralized by some counteracting factor. Such is the case with crime. The wrong done to society is annulled by the penalty which is meted out, if it functions properly. Since the evil that was implied is never produced, the positive relations in these fundamental conditions of society are strengthened. Yet it is rendered inoffensive in spite of itself, so to speak, and the sentiments of aversion which it arouses are well grounded.

effect. These relationships can then be transformed, by an equally logical operation, into rules of action for the future. What critics have called our "positivism" is only one certain aspect of this rationalism.[2]

For purposes of prediction and interpretation one may be permitted to disregard certain facts, but only to the extent that they are judged irrelevant. When they are correctly understood, facts are as basic in science as in practical life: in science because there is nothing to be gained by looking behind them to speculate on their reason for being, and in practical life since their very usefulness is their only justification. It therefore seems to us that in these times of renascent mysticism an undertaking such as ours should be regarded quite without apprehension and even with sympathy by all those who, while disagreeing with us on certain points, yet share our faith in the future of reason.

[2] That is, it must not be confused with the positivistic metaphysics of Comte and Spencer.

AUTHOR'S PREFACE TO THE
SECOND EDITION

When this book appeared for the first time, it aroused lively controversy. Current thought, shaken out of itself, resisted at first so loudly that for a time it was almost impossible for us to make ourselves heard. On the very points on which we had expressed ourselves most explicitly, views were freely attributed to us which had nothing in common with our own; and our opponents held that they were refuting us in refuting these mistaken ideas. Whereas we had declared repeatedly that the individual consciousness was for us not material, but only a more or less systematized aggregate of phenomena, we were charged with realism and with ontologism. Whereas we had expressly stated and reiterated that social life is constituted wholly of collective "representations,"[1] we were accused of eliminating the mental element from sociology. Our critics even went so far as to resurrect old controversies which we had supposed long settled. They imputed to us certain opinions that we had never upheld, under the plea of their being "in conformity with our principles." Fortunately, experience has demonstrated the weakness of such attacks, since the arbitrary methods by which these critics have supposedly reconstructed our system permits an easy refutation.

We believe we are not deceiving ourselves in saying that

[1] [This word, *représentations*, which might be translated "ideas" (cf. the German *Vorstellungen*), is used by M. Durkheim in a technical sense, essential to his sociological theory. See C. E. Gehlke, *Émile Durkheim's Contributions to Sociological Theory* (1915), p. 17.—EDITOR.]

the opposition has been growing progressively weaker. Of course, more than one proposition is still contested, and we could show neither surprise nor regret at such healthy salutary controversy. It is natural to expect that our formulas will be revised in the future. A product of individual and necessarily limited experience, we expect them to develop in proportion as we acquire a more extended and profound knowledge of social reality. Moreover, in this matter of method, one can establish only provisional rules, since methods, too, will change as science advances. It is nonetheless true that, in recent years, in spite of opposition, the cause of objective, specific, and methodological sociology has gained ground continuously. The founding of the *Année sociologique* has certainly contributed much to this result. Because it embraces the entire field of the science, the *Année* has been able, better than any more limited enterprise, to establish a standard which sociology must, and will, achieve. We have seen that sociology is not destined to remain a branch of general philosophy, and also that it can treat facts in detail without degenerating into empty erudition. We cannot pay too great homage to the ardor and devotion of our collaborators; it is because of them that we have been able to envisage the position of our science and cultivate its possibilities.

However real this progress is, we are also aware that the mistakes and confusions of the past are not yet entirely dissipated. It is for this reason that we should like, on the occasion of this second edition, to add a few explanations to all those we have already given, to answer certain criticisms, and to give added precision to certain points.

I

The proposition which states that social facts are to be treated as things—the proposition at the very basis of our method—is one of those which have provoked most contradiction. It has been considered not only paradoxical but ridiculous for us to compare the realities of the social world with those of the external world. But our critics have curiously misinterpreted the meaning and import of this analogy, for it was not our intention to reduce the higher to the lower forms of being, but merely to claim for the higher forms a degree of reality at least equal to that which is readily granted to the lower. We assert not that social facts are material things but that they are things by the same right as material things, although they differ from them in type.

What, precisely, is a "thing"? A thing differs from an idea in the same way as that which we know from without differs from that which we know from within. Things include all objects of knowledge that cannot be conceived by purely mental activity, those that require for their conception data from outside the mind, from observations and experiments, those which are built up from the more external and immediately accessible characteristics to the less visible and more profound. To treat the facts of a certain order as things is not, then, to place them in a certain category of reality but to assume a certain mental attitude toward them on the principle that when approaching their study we are absolutely ignorant of their nature, and that their characteristic properties, like the unknown causes on which they depend, cannot be discovered by even the most careful introspection.

With the terms thus defined, our proposition, far from

being a paradox, could almost pass for a truism if it were not too often misinterpreted in the human sciences and especially in sociology. One might even say in this sense that, with the possible exception of mathematical units, every object of science is a thing. In mathematics, to proceed from the simplest to the most complex concepts we need only our own mental processes and analyses; but in the case of "facts" properly so called, these are, at the moment when we undertake to study them scientifically, necessarily unknown things of which we are ignorant; and any "representations" which we have been able to make of them in the course of our life, having been made without method and criticism, are devoid of scientific value, and must be distinguished from the scientific mentality. The facts of individual psychology are excellent examples of this distinction, for although they are by definition purely mental, yet the consciousness we have of them reveals to us neither their nature nor their genesis. It permits us to know them up to a certain point, just as our sensations give us a certain familiarity with heat or light, sound or electricity; it gives us confused, fleeting, subjective impressions of them but no clear and scientific notions or explanatory concepts. It is precisely for this reason that there has been founded in the course of this century an objective psychology whose fundamental purpose is to study mental facts from the outside, that is, as things.

Such a procedure is all the more necessary with social facts, for consciousness is even more helpless in knowing them than in knowing its own life.[2] The objection will be

---

[2] To allow our first proposition, that social facts must be treated as things, it is not necessary to maintain that social life consists of other than "representations"; it is sufficient to postulate that the "representations," individual or collective, can be studied scientifically only if they are studied objectively.

raised that, since social facts are our own personal constructs, we have only to resort to introspection in order to
determine what we put into them and how we formed them.
But we must remember that the greater part of our social
institutions was bequeathed to us by former generations.
We ourselves took no part in their formation, and consequently we cannot by introspection discover the causes
which brought them about. Furthermore, even when we
have collaborated in their genesis, we can only with difficulty
obtain even a confused and inexact insight into the true
nature of our action and the causes which determined it.
When it is simply a matter of our private acts, we know very
imperfectly the relatively simple motives that guide us. We
believe ourselves disinterested when we act egoistically; we
think we are motivated by hate when we are yielding to love,
and obeying reason when we are the slaves of unreasoned
prejudices, etc. How, then, should we have the faculty of
discerning with greater clarity the causes, otherwise complex, from which collective acts proceed? For, at the very
least, each one of us participates in them only as an infinitesimal unit; we have a multitude of collaborators, and
what takes place in other consciousnesses escapes us.

Our principle, then, implies no metaphysical conception,
no speculation about the fundamental nature of beings.
What it demands is that the sociologist put himself in the
same state of mind as the physicist, chemist, or physiologist
when he probes into a still unexplored region of the scientific
domain. When he penetrates the social world, he must be
aware that he is penetrating the unknown; he must feel himself in the presence of facts whose laws are as unsuspected as
were those of life before the era of biology; he must be prepared for discoveries which will surprise and disturb him.

Sociology is far from having arrived at this degree of intellectual maturity. While the scientist who studies physical nature is very keenly aware of the resistance it offers him, and which he has so much difficulty in overcoming, the sociologist seems to move in a sphere perfectly transparent to his view, so great is the ease with which the most obscure questions are resolved. In the present state of the science we really do not even know what are the principal social institutions, such as the state, or the family; what is the right of property or contract, of punishment and responsibility. We are almost completely ignorant of the factors on which they depend, the functions they fulfil, the laws of their development; we are scarcely beginning to shed even a glimmer of light on some of these points. Yet one has only to glance through the works on sociology to see how rare is the appreciation of this ignorance and these difficulties. Not only do social theorists consider themselves at once obliged to dogmatize on all problems, but they find themselves able to set forth in a few pages or phrases the very essence of the most complex phenomena. Theorizing of this sort cannot have its source in facts, for facts could not be so quickly disposed of; it springs from the prejudices which the author held prior to his research. To be sure, each man's individual conception of what our social customs are, or what they ought to be, is itself a factor in their development. But these conceptions in turn are additional facts which must be properly identified and studied objectively. The important thing to know is not the way in which a certain thinker individually conceives a certain institution but the group's conception of it; this conception alone is socially significant. Nor can this conception be arrived at by simple introspection, since it does not exist in its entirety in any one individual; we must find external objective signs that will make it perceptible. Further, even a product of spontaneous generation is in itself an effect of external causes which must also be determined in order to estimate its role in the future. Ultimately, we must always return to the same method.

II

Another proposition has been argued no less vehemently than the preceding one, namely, that social phenomena are external to individuals. Today our critics grant, willingly enough, that the facts of individual and of collective life are not altogether coterminous; one can even say that a quite general, if not unanimous, understanding on this point is in process of being achieved. Practically all sociologists now demand a separate existence for their science; but because society is composed only of individuals,[3] the common-sense view still holds that sociology is a superstructure built upon the substratum of the individual consciousness and that otherwise it would be suspended in a social vacuum.

What is so readily judged inadmissible in the matter of social facts is freely admitted in the other realms of nature. Whenever certain elements combine and thereby produce, by the fact of their combination, new phenomena, it is plain that these new phenomena reside not in the original elements but in the totality formed by their union. The living cell contains nothing but mineral particles, as society contains nothing but individuals. Yet it is patently impossible for the phenomena characteristic of life to reside in the atoms of hydrogen, oxygen, carbon, and nitrogen. How

---

[3] The proposition is only partially exact. In addition to the individuals there are also certain integrating elements of society. It is true merely that individuals are the only active elements therein.

could the properties of life exist in inanimate elements? How would the biological properties be divided among these elements? These properties could not exist equally in all the elements because the latter are dissimilar by nature; carbon is not nitrogen and consequently cannot have the same properties as nitrogen or function in the same way. It is equally inadmissible that each of the principal characteristics of life be resident in a certain group of atoms. Life could not be thus separated into discrete parts; it is a unit, and consequently its substratum can be only the living substance in its totality and not the element parts of which it is composed. The inanimate particles of the cell do not assimilate food, reproduce, and, in a word, live; only the cell itself as a unit can achieve these functions.

What we say of life could be repeated for all possible compounds. The hardness of bronze is not in the copper, the tin, or the lead, which are its ingredients and which are soft and malleable bodies; it is in their mixture. The fluidity of water and its nutritional and other properties are not to be found in the two gases of which it is composed but in the complex substance which they form by their association.

Let us apply this principle to sociology. If, as we may say, this synthesis constituting every society yields new phenomena, differing from those which take place in individual consciousnesses, we must, indeed, admit that these facts reside exclusively in the very society itself which produces them, and not in its parts, i.e., its members. They are, then, in this sense external to individual consciousnesses, considered as such, just as the distinctive characteristics of life are external to the mineral substances composing the living being. These new phenomena cannot be reduced to their elements without contradiction in terms, since, by definition, they presuppose something different from the

properties of these elements. Thus we have a new justification for the separation which we have established between
psychology, which is properly the science of the mind of the
individual, and sociology.

Social facts do not differ from psychological facts in quality only: *they have a different substratum;* they evolve in a
different milieu; and they depend on different conditions.
This does not mean that they are not also mental after a
fashion, since they all consist of ways of thinking or behaving. But the states of the collective consciousness are different in nature from the states of the individual consciousness; they are "representations" of another type. The
mentality of groups is not the same as that of individuals; it
has its own laws. The two sciences are thus as clearly distinct as two sciences can be, whatever relationships there
may otherwise be between them.

Nevertheless, on this point we may make a distinction
which will perhaps throw some light on the discussion.

That the substance of social life cannot be explained by
purely psychological factors, i.e., by the states of the individual consciousness, seems to us to be most evident. Indeed, what the collective representations convey is the way
in which the group conceives itself in its relation to objects
which affect it. The group differs from the individual in its
constitution, and the things that affect it are therefore of a
different nature. Representations or concepts that reflect
neither the same objects nor the same subjects cannot be
traced to the same causes. To understand the way in
which a society thinks of itself and of its environment one
must consider the nature of the society and not that of the
individuals. Even the symbols which express these conceptions change according to the type of society.

If, for example, it claims descent from a totemic animal,

it is conceived as one of those special groups called "clans." If the animal is replaced by a human, but equally mythical, ancestor, this concept of the clan must also be modified. If, over and above local or family divinities, it postulates others on which it believes itself to be dependent, it follows that the local and family groups of which it is composed have tended to concentrate and unite, and the degree of unity which the divinities present corresponds to the degree of unity attained at the same moment by the society. If the clan condemns certain modes of conduct, it is because they violate certain of its fundamental sentiments which are derived from its constitution, as those of the individual derive from his physical temperament and his mental organization. Thus, even if individual psychology had no more secrets for us, it could not give us the solution for any of these problems, since they relate to orders of facts concerning which it can have nothing to offer.

With this distinction in mind one can ask whether individual and social representations do not, nevertheless, resemble each other in that both are equally "representations"; and whether in consequence of these resemblances, certain abstract laws would not be common to the two realms. Myths, popular legends, religious conceptions of all sorts, moral beliefs, etc., reflect a reality different from the individual's reality; but the way in which they attract and repel each other, unite or separate, may nevertheless be independent of their content and may depend uniquely on their general quality as representations. Although their substance is different, they would behave in their mutual relations as do sensations, images, or ideas, in the individual. Is it not conceivable, for example, that contiguity and resemblance, logical contrasts and antagonisms, act in the same way, whatever may be the things they represent? Thus we arrive at the idea of the possibility of an entirely formal psychology which would be a sort of common ground for individual psychology and for sociology, and this perhaps explains the reluctance of certain scholars to distinguish too sharply between the two sciences.

Strictly speaking, in the present state of our knowledge the question thus stated could not receive a categorical solution. On the other hand, all that we know about the way in which individual ideas combine reduces itself to those few very general and vague propositions commonly called the "laws of the association of ideas." As for the laws of collective thinking, they are still more completely unknown. Social psychology, whose task it is to determine these laws, is scarcely more than a name, without a definite subject matter, and including all sorts of generalities, diverse and inexact. We need to investigate, by comparison of mythical themes, popular legends, traditions, and languages, the manner in which social representations adhere to and repel one another, how they fuse or separate from one another, etc. This problem perhaps merits the curiosity of investigators, but it has scarcely been approached by them; and so long as not even a few of these laws have been discovered, it will evidently be impossible to determine with certainty whether or not they parallel those of individual psychology. In the absence of such certitude it is, at the very least, probable that, even if resemblances do exist between these two sorts of laws, the differences are also nonetheless marked.

It appears quite improbable that the stuff of which representations are made should have no influence on their manner of combining. It is true that psychologists sometimes speak of the laws of the association of ideas as if they were the same for all species of individual representations. But nothing is less probable: images do not compound among themselves like sensations, nor concepts like images. If psychology were more advanced, it would doubtless find that each category of mental states has formal laws which are peculiar to it. If such is the case, we must with all the more reason expect that the corresponding laws of social thought will be as distinctive as this thought itself. Even with the little experience we have had with this class of facts, it is difficult not to perceive their distinctiveness. This peculiarity will explain the apparently strange combinations and segregations of religious ideas (which certainly are collective in origin) and their transformations which produce compounds of contradictory elements widely different from the ordinary products of individual thought. If, then, we may assume that certain laws of social thinking actually are similar to certain laws of individual psychology, it is not because the former are simply a particular case of the latter but because, in spite of the differences, which are certainly important, there may still be similarities which abstraction may discover but which are still unknown.

In no case can sociology simply·borrow from psychology any one of its principles in order to apply it, as such, to social facts. Collective thought, in its form as in its matter, must be studied in its entirety, in and for itself, with an understanding of its peculiar nature. How much it resembles the thought of individuals must be left for future investigation. It is a problem which is rather within the jurisdiction of general philosophy and abstract logic than in the science of social facts.[4]

III

In our first chapter we gave a definition of social facts as ways of acting or thinking with the peculiar characteristic of exercising a coercive influence on individual consciousnesses. Confusion has arisen on this score which requires comment.

Scholars are so accustomed to apply the forms of philosophical thought to sociological matters that they are prone to see in this preliminary definition a kind of philosophy of social phenomena. They claimed that we were explaining social phenomena by constraint, just as Tarde explains them by imitation. This was far from our intention—in fact, it had never even occurred to us that it could have been so interpreted, so much is it contrary to our entire method. We proposed not to anticipate the conclusions of sociological science by a philosophical view but simply to indicate by what external signs it is possible to recognize the facts of which it must treat in order that the student may know how to detect them and in order that he may not confuse them with others. It was a matter of restricting the field of research as closely as possible, not of subsuming it under a sort of all-embracing intuitive principle. We are very glad to discuss the criticism directed against this definition because it did not include all the characteristics of the social fact and consequently was not the only possible definition.

[4] It is superfluous to show how, from this point of view, the necessity of studying facts objectively becomes all the more evident since they result from syntheses which take place outside us and of which we have not even that confused perception which consciousness can give us of internal phenomena.

Quite obviously the social fact may be characterized in several different ways, and there is no reason why any one certain distinctive characteristic should be attached to it oftener than any other.[5] It is only important to choose that characteristic which appears the best for one's purpose; and it is even quite possible to use, concurrently, several criteria, according to the circumstances. This is what we ourselves have occasionally found necessary in sociology; for there are cases where the character of constraint is not easily recognizable. Since we are here concerned with an initial definition, it is necessary only that the criteria we use be immediately discernible and relevant to the intended research. These considerations have not been manifest in the definitions that have at times been opposed to ours. Critics have said, for example, that the social fact is "all that takes place in and through society," or again, "what interests and affects the group in some way." But only when the science is already advanced can one determine whether or not society is the cause of a fact, or whether this fact has social effects. Such definitions could not therefore serve to determine the subject matter of the investigation at its beginning.

[5] The coercive power that we attribute to it is so far from being the whole of the social fact that it can present the opposite character equally well. Institutions may impose themselves upon us, but we cling to them; they compel us, and we love them; they constrain us, and we find our welfare in our adherence to them and in this very constraint. The moralists have often pointed out the same antithesis between the two concepts of "the good" and of "duty," which present two different and equally real aspects of the moral life. There is perhaps no collective behavior which does not exercise this double action upon us, and it is contradictory in appearance only. If we have not previously described social facts in terms of this double functioning —parallel to the moral concepts of "good" and "duty"—it is because the objective manifestations are not easily perceptible. The "good" is somewhat more subjective, more intimate, than "duty," and consequently less easily grasped.

In order that these definitions may be utilized, the study of social facts must already have made considerable progress, and consequently one must have discovered earlier some other means of finding and identifying them.

While with some critics our definition has been found too narrow, it has likewise been accused of being too wide and embracing almost the whole of reality. In fact, it has been said that every physical milieu exercises constraint on the beings which are subject to its action; for they are compelled, in a certain measure, to adapt themselves to it. But between these two modes of coercion there is all the difference which separates the physical from the social milieu. The pressure exerted by one or several bodies on other bodies, or even on human wills, cannot be confused with that which the consciousness of a group exercises on the consciousnesses of its members. The peculiar characteristic of social constraint is that it is due, not to the rigidity of certain molecular arrangements, but to the prestige with which certain representations are invested. It is true that habits, either physical or social, have in certain respects this same feature. They dominate us and impose beliefs and practices upon us. But they rule us from within, for they are in every case an integral part of ourself. On the contrary, social beliefs and practices act on us from without; thus the influence exerted by them differs fundamentally from the effect of habit.

We must not be surprised, moreover, if other phenomena of nature display the very characteristic by which we have defined social phenomena. This parallelism arises chiefly from the fact that both are real things. For everything that is real has a definite nature that asserts control, that must be taken into account and is never completely overcome, even when we succeed in neutralizing it. And, fundamentally, this is the very essence of the idea of social constraint; for it merely implies that collective ways of acting or thinking have a reality outside the individuals who, at every moment of time, conform to it. These ways of thinking and acting exist in their own right. The individual finds them completely formed, and he cannot evade or change them. He is therefore obliged to reckon with them. It is difficult (we do not say impossible) for him to modify them in direct proportion to the extent that they share in the material and moral supremacy of society over its members. Of course, the individual plays a role in their genesis. But in order that there may be a social fact, several individuals, at the very least, must have contributed their action; and in this joint activity is the origin of a new fact. Since this joint activity takes place outside each one of us (for a plurality of consciousnesses enters into it), its necessary effect is to fix, to institute outside us, certain ways of acting and certain judgments which do not depend on each particular will taken separately. It has been pointed out[6] that the word "institution" well expresses this special mode of reality, provided that the ordinary significance of it be slightly extended. One can, indeed, without distorting the meaning of this expression, designate as "institutions" all the beliefs and all the modes of conduct instituted by the collectivity. Sociology can then be defined as the science of institutions, of their genesis and of their functioning.[7]

[6] See the article "Sociology," in the *Grande encyclopédie*, by MM. Fauconnet and Mauss.

[7] Because beliefs and social practices thus come to us from without, it does not follow that we receive them passively or without modification. In reflecting on collective institutions and assimilating them for ourselves, we

It is unnecessary to dwell upon the other controversies that this work aroused, for they touch on nothing that is essential. The general import of our method does not depend on the procedures that one happens to employ either in the classification of social types or in distinguishing between normal and pathological social facts. Very often the disagreements were due to the refusal to admit at all, or to admit with reservations, our fundamental principle, the objective reality of social facts. Ultimately, everything rests on this principle and grows out of it. For this reason it has seemed useful to us once more to bring it out in full relief, separating it from all secondary considerations. And we are certain that, in attributing to it such dominating importance, we are remaining true to sociological tradition; for it is upon this principle fundamentally that all sociology has been built. This science, indeed, could be brought into existence only with the realization that social phenomena, although immaterial, are nevertheless real things, the proper objects of scientific study. To be convinced that their investigation was legitimate, it was necessary to assume that they had a definite and permanent existence, that they do not depend on individual caprice, and that they give rise to uniform and orderly relations. Thus the history of sociology

---

individualize them and impart to them more or less personal characteristics. Similarly, in reflecting on the physical world, each of us colors it after his own fashion, and different individuals adapt themselves differently to the same physical environment. It is for this reason that each one of us creates, in a measure, his own morality, religion, and mode of life. There is no conformity to social convention that does not comprise an entire range of individual shades. It is nonetheless true that this field of variations is a limited one. It verges on nonexistence or is very restricted in that circle of religious and moral affairs where deviation easily becomes crime. It is wider in all that concerns economic life. But, sooner or later, even in the latter instance, one encounters the limit that cannot be crossed.

is but a long endeavor to give this principle precision, to deepen it, and to develop all the consequences it implies. In spite of the great advances which have been made in this direction, it will be clear, from what follows in this work, that numerous survivals of the anthropocentric bias still remain and that here, as elsewhere, they bar the way to science. It displeases man to renounce the unlimited power over the social order he has so long attributed to himself; and on the other hand, it seems to him that, if collective forces really exist, he is necessarily obliged to submit to them without being able to modify them. This makes him inclined to deny their existence. In vain have repeated experiences taught him that this omnipotence, the illusion of which he complacently entertains, has always been a cause of weakness in him; that his power over things really began only when he recognized that they have a nature of their own, and resigned himself to learning this nature from them. Rejected by all other sciences, this deplorable prejudice stubbornly maintains itself in sociology. Nothing is more urgent than to liberate our science from it, and this is the principal purpose of our efforts.

AUTHOR'S INTRODUCTION

Until the present, sociologists have given little thought to describing and defining the method they employ in the study of social facts. Thus, in the entire work of Spencer the problem of methodology occupies no place, for *The Study of Sociology*, perhaps a misleading title, is devoted to demonstrating the difficulties and possibilities of sociology, not to expounding the methods it ought to use. Mill, it is true, has dealt at great length with the question;[1] but he has only refined with his dialectics what Comte had already expounded, without adding anything really original. A chapter in the *Cours de philosophie positive*[2] is, then, almost the only original and important study we have on the matter.

This apparent neglect need not surprise us; for the great sociologists whose names we have just recalled seldom advanced beyond vague generalities on the nature of societies, on the relations between the social and the biological realms, and on the general march of progress. Even the voluminous sociology of Spencer has scarcely any other purpose than to show how the law of universal evolution applies to human societies. Certainly no special and complex methods are required for the treatment of these philosophical questions. Sociologists have been content, therefore, to compare the merits of deduction and induction and to make a superficial inquiry into the most general means and methods at the command of the sociological investigators. But the precautions to be taken in the observation of facts, the manner in

[1] *System of Logic* (1st ed.), Vol. VI, chaps. vii–xii.
[2] See 2d ed., pp. 294–336.

which the principal problems should be formulated, the direction research should take, the specific methods of work which may enable it to reach its conclusions—all these remained completely undetermined.

A happy combination of circumstances, among the most important of which may rightly be placed the proposal to establish a regular course in sociology in the Faculty of Letters at Bordeaux, enabled us to devote ourselves early to the study of social science and, indeed, to make it our vocation. Therefore, we have been able to abandon these very general questions and to attack a certain number of definite problems. The very force of events has thus led us to construct a method that is, we believe, more precise and more exactly adapted to the distinctive characteristics of social phenomena. We wish here to expound the results of our work in applied sociology in their entirety and to submit them for discussion. They are, of course, contained by implication in the book which we published recently on the *Division in Social Labor*. But it seems to us that it is of some advantage to make them explicit and to give them separate formulation, accompanying them with proofs and illustrations drawn either from that work or from works still unpublished. The public will thus be better able to judge of the direction we are trying to give to sociological studies.

CHAPTER I
WHAT IS A SOCIAL FACT?

Before inquiring into the method suited to the study of social facts, it is important to know which facts are commonly called "social." This information is all the more necessary since the designation "social" is used with little precision. It is currently employed for practically all phenomena generally diffused within society, however small their social interest. But on that basis, there are, as it were, no human events that may not be called social. Each individual drinks, sleeps, eats, reasons; and it is to society's interest that these functions be exercised in an orderly manner. If, then, all these facts are counted as "social" facts, sociology would have no subject matter exclusively its own, and its domain would be confused with that of biology and psychology.

But in reality there is in every society a certain group of phenomena which may· be differentiated from those studied by the other natural sciences. When I fulfil my obligations as brother, husband, or citizen, when I execute my contracts, I perform duties which are defined, externally to myself and my acts, in law and in custom. Even if they conform to my own sentiments and I feel their reality subjectively, such reality is still objective, for I did not create them; I merely inherited them through my education. How many times it happens, moreover, that we are ignorant of the details of the obligations incumbent upon us, and that in order to acquaint ourselves with them we must consult the law and its authorized interpreters! Similarly, the church-member finds the beliefs and practices of his religious life ready-made at birth; their existence prior to his own implies their existence outside of himself. The system of signs I use to express my thought, the system of currency I employ to pay my debts, the instruments of credit I utilize in my commercial relations, the practices followed in my profession, etc., function independently of my own use of them. And these statements can be repeated for each member of society. Here, then, are ways of acting, thinking, and feeling that present the noteworthy property of existing outside the individual consciousness.

These types of conduct or thought are not only external to the individual but are, moreover, endowed with coercive power, by virtue of which they impose themselves upon him, independent of his individual will. Of course, when I fully consent and conform to them, this constraint is felt only slightly, if at all, and is therefore unnecessary. But it is, nonetheless, an intrinsic characteristic of these facts, the proof thereof being that it asserts itself as soon as I attempt to resist it. If I attempt to violate the law, it reacts against me so as to prevent my act before its accomplishment, or to nullify my violation by restoring the damage, if it is accomplished and reparable, or to make me expiate it if it cannot be compensated for otherwise.

In the case of purely moral maxims, the public conscience exercises a check on every act which offends it by means of the surveillance it exercises over the conduct of citizens, and the appropriate penalties at its disposal. In many cases the constraint is less violent, but nevertheless it always exists. If I do not submit to the conventions of society, if in my dress I do not conform to the customs observed in my country and in my class, the ridicule I provoke, the social

isolation in which I am kept, produce, although in an attenuated form, the same effects as a punishment in the strict
sense of the word. The constraint is nonetheless efficacious
for being indirect. I am not obliged to speak French with
my fellow-countrymen nor to use the legal currency, but I
cannot possibly do otherwise. If I tried to escape this necessity, my attempt would fail miserably. As an industrialist,
I am free to apply the technical methods of former centuries;
but by doing so, I should invite certain ruin. Even when I
free myself from these rules and violate them successfully,
I am always compelled to struggle with them. When finally
overcome, they make their constraining power sufficiently
felt by the resistance they offer. The enterprises of all in-
novators, including successful ones, come up against resistance of this kind.

Here, then, is a category of facts with very distinctive
characteristics: it consists of ways of acting, thinking, and
feeling, external to the individual, and endowed with a
power of coercion, by reason of which they control him.
These ways of thinking could not be confused with biological
phenomena, since they consist of representations and of
actions; nor with psychological phenomena, which exist only
in the individual consciousness and through it. They constitute, thus, a new variety of phenomena; and it is to them
exclusively that the term "social" ought to be applied. And
this term fits them quite well, for it is clear that, since their
source is not in the individual, their substratum can be no
other than society, either the political society as a whole or
some one of the partial groups it includes, such as religious
denominations, political, literary, and occupational associa-
tions, etc. On the other hand, this term "social" applies to
them exclusively, for it has a distinct meaning only if it

designates exclusively the phenomena which are not included in any of the categories of facts that have already been established and classified. These ways of thinking and acting therefore constitute the proper domain of sociology. It is true that, when we define them with this word "constraint," we risk shocking the zealous partisans of absolute individualism. For those who profess the complete autonomy of the individual, man's dignity is diminished whenever he is made to feel that he is not completely self-determinant. It is generally accepted today, however, that most of our ideas and our tendencies are not developed by ourselves but come to us from without. How can they become a part of us except by imposing themselves upon us? This is the whole meaning of our definition. And it is generally accepted, moreover, that social constraint is not necessarily incompatible with the individual personality.[1]

Since the examples that we have just cited (legal and moral regulations, religious faiths, financial systems, etc.) all consist of established beliefs and practices, one might be led to believe that social facts exist only where there is some social organization. But there are other facts without such crystallized form which have the same objectivity and the same ascendency over the individual. These are called "social currents." Thus the great movements of enthusiasm, indignation, and pity in a crowd do not originate in any one of the particular individual consciousnesses. They come to each one of us from without and can carry us away in spite of ourselves. Of course, it may happen that, in abandoning myself to them unreservedly, I do not feel the pressure they exert upon me. But it is revealed as soon as I try to resist

---

[1] We do not intend to imply, however, that all constraint is normal. We shall return to this point later.

them. Let an individual attempt to oppose one of these collective manifestations, and the emotions that he denies will turn against him. Now, if this power of external coercion asserts itself so clearly in cases of resistance, it must exist also in the first-mentioned cases, although we are unconscious of it. We are then victims of the illusion of having ourselves created that which actually forced itself from without. If the complacency with which we permit ourselves to be carried along conceals the pressure undergone, nevertheless it does not abolish it. Thus, air is no less heavy because we do not detect its weight. So, even if we ourselves have spontaneously contributed to the production of the common emotion, the impression we have received differs markedly from that which we would have experienced if we had been alone. Also, once the crowd has dispersed, that is, once these social influences have ceased to act upon us and we are alone again, the emotions which have passed through the mind appear strange to us, and we no longer recognize them as ours. We realize that these feelings have been impressed upon us to a much greater extent than they were created by us. It may even happen that they horrify us, so much were they contrary to our nature. Thus, a group of individuals, most of whom are perfectly inoffensive, may, when gathered in a crowd, be drawn into acts of atrocity. And what we say of these transitory outbursts applies similarly to those more permanent currents of opinion on religious, political, literary, or artistic matters which are constantly being formed around us, whether in society as a whole or in more limited circles.

To confirm this definition of the social fact by a characteristic illustration from common experience, one need only observe the manner in which children are brought up. Considering the facts as they are and as they have always been, it becomes immediately evident that all education is a continuous effort to impose on the child ways of seeing, feeling, and acting which he could not have arrived at spontaneously. From the very first hours of his life, we compel him to eat, drink, and sleep at regular hours; we constrain him to cleanliness, calmness, and obedience; later we exert pressure upon him in order that he may learn proper consideration for others, respect for customs and conventions, the need for work, etc. If, in time, this constraint ceases to be felt, it is because it gradually gives rise to habits and to internal tendencies that render constraint unnecessary; but nevertheless it is not abolished, for it is still the source from which these habits were derived. It is true that, according to Spencer, a rational education ought to reject such methods, allowing the child to act in complete liberty; but as this pedagogic theory has never been applied by any known people, it must be accepted only as an expression of personal opinion, not as a fact which can contradict the aforementioned observations. What makes these facts particularly instructive is that the aim of education is, precisely, the socialization of the human being; the process of education, therefore, gives us in a nutshell the historical fashion in which the social being is constituted. This unremitting pressure to which the child is subjected is the very pressure of the social milieu which tends to fashion him in its own image, and of which parents and teachers are merely the representatives and intermediaries.

It follows that sociological phenomena cannot be defined by their universality. A thought which we find in every individual consciousness, a movement repeated by all individuals, is not thereby a social fact. If sociologists have been satisfied with defining them by this characteristic, it is because they confused them with what one might call their reincarnation in the individual. It is, however, the collective aspects of the beliefs, tendencies, and practices of a group that characterize truly social phenomena. As for the forms that the collective states assume when refracted in the individual, these are things of another sort. This duality is clearly demonstrated by the fact that these two orders of phenomena are frequently found dissociated from one another. Indeed, certain of these social manners of acting and thinking acquire, by reason of their repetition, a certain rigidity which on its own account crystallizes them, so to speak, and isolates them from the particular events which reflect them. They thus acquire a body, a tangible form, and constitute a reality in their own right, quite distinct from the individual facts which produce it. Collective habits are inherent not only in the successive acts which they determine but, by a privilege of which we find no example in the biological realm, they are given permanent expression in a formula which is repeated from mouth to mouth, transmitted by education, and fixed even in writing. Such is the origin and nature of legal and moral rules, popular aphorisms and proverbs, articles of faith wherein religious or political groups condense their beliefs, standards of taste established by literary schools, etc. None of these can be found entirely reproduced in the applications made of them by individuals, since they can exist even without being actually applied.

No doubt, this dissociation does not always manifest itself with equal distinctness, but its obvious existence in the important and numerous cases just cited is sufficient to prove that the social fact is a thing distinct from its individual manifestations. Moreover, even when this dissociation is not immediately apparent, it may often be disclosed by certain devices of method. Such dissociation is indispensable if one wishes to separate social facts from their alloys in order to observe them in a state of purity. Currents of opinion, with an intensity varying according to the time and place, impel certain groups either to more marriages, for example, or to more suicides, or to a higher or lower birthrate, etc. These currents are plainly social facts. At first sight they seem inseparable from the forms they take in individual cases. But statistics furnish us with the means of isolating them. They are, in fact, represented with considerable exactness by the rates of births, marriages, and suicides, that is, by the number obtained by dividing the average annual total of marriages, births, suicides, by the number of persons whose ages lie within the range in which marriages, births, and suicides occur.[2] Since each of these figures contains all the individual cases indiscriminately, the individual circumstances which may have had a share in the production of the phenomenon are neutralized and, consequently, do not contribute to its determination. The average, then, expresses a certain state of the group mind (*l'âme collective*).

Such are social phenomena, when disentangled from all foreign matter. As for their individual manifestations, these are indeed, to a certain extent, social, since they partly reproduce a social model. Each of them also depends, and to a large extent, on the organopsychological constitution of the individual and on the particular circumstances in which he is placed. Thus they are not sociological phenomena in the strict sense of the word. They belong to two realms at once; one could call them sociopsychological. They interest

---

[2] Suicides do not occur at every age, and they take place with varying intensity at the different ages in which they occur.

the sociologist without constituting the immediate subject matter of sociology. There exist in the interior of organisms similar phenomena, compound in their nature, which form in their turn the subject matter of the "hybrid sciences," such as physiological chemistry, for example.

The objection may be raised that a phenomenon is collective only if it is common to all members of society, or at least to most of them—in other words, if it is truly general. This may be true; but it is general because it is collective (that is, more or less obligatory), and certainly not collective because general. It is a group condition repeated in the individual because imposed on him. It is to be found in each part because it exists in the whole, rather than in the whole because it exists in the parts. This becomes conspicuously evident in those beliefs and practices which are transmitted to us ready-made by previous generations; we receive and adopt them because, being both collective and ancient, they are invested with a particular authority that education has taught us to recognize and respect. It is, of course, true that a vast portion of our social culture is transmitted to us in this way; but even when the social fact is due in part to our direct collaboration, its nature is not different. A collective emotion which bursts forth suddenly and violently in a crowd does not express merely what all the individual sentiments had in common; it is something entirely different, as we have shown. It results from their being together, a product of the actions and reactions which take place between individual consciousnesses; and if each individual consciousness echoes the collective sentiment, it is by virtue of the special energy resident in its collective origin. If all hearts beat in unison, this is not the result of a spontaneous and pre-established harmony but rather because an identical force propels them in the same direction. Each is carried along by all.

We thus arrive at the point where we can formulate and delimit in a precise way the domain of sociology. It comprises only a limited group of phenomena. A social fact is to be recognized by the power of external coercion which it exercises or is capable of exercising over individuals, and the presence of this power may be recognized in its turn either by the existence of some specific sanction or by the resistance offered against every individual effort that tends to violate it. One can, however, define it also by its diffusion within the group, provided that, in conformity with our previous remarks, one takes care to add as a second and essential characteristic that its own existence is independent of the individual forms it assumes in its diffusion. This last criterion is perhaps, in certain cases, easier to apply than the preceding one. In fact, the constraint is easy to ascertain when it expresses itself externally by some direct reaction of society, as is the case in law, morals, beliefs, customs, and even fashions. But when it is only indirect, like the constraint which an economic organization exercises, it cannot always be so easily detected. Generality combined with externality may, then, be easier to establish. Moreover, this second definition is but another form of the first; for if a mode of behavior whose existence is external to individual consciousnesses becomes general, this can only be brought about by its being imposed upon them.[3]

[3] It will be seen how this definition of the social fact diverges from that which forms the basis of the ingenious system of M. Tarde. First of all, we wish to state that our researches have nowhere led us to observe that preponderant influence in the genesis of collective facts which M. Tarde attributes to imitation. Moreover, from the preceding definition, which is not a theory but simply a résumé of the immediate data of observation, it

But these several phenomena present the same characteristic by which we defined the others. These "ways of existing" are imposed on the individual precisely in the same fashion as the "ways of acting" of which we have spoken. Indeed, when we wish to know how a society is divided politically, of what these divisions themselves are composed, and how complete is the fusion existing between them, we shall not achieve our purpose by physical inspection and by geographical observations; for these phenomena are social, even when they have some basis in physical nature. It is only by a study of public law that a comprehension of this organization is possible, for it is this law that determines the organization, as it equally determines our domestic and civil relations. This political organization is, then, no less obligatory than the social facts mentioned above. If the population crowds into our cities instead of scattering into the country, this is due to a trend of public opinion, a collective drive that imposes this concentration upon the individuals. We can no more choose the style of our houses than of our clothing—at least, both are equally obligatory. The channels of communication prescribe the direction of internal migrations and commerce, etc., and

seems indeed to follow, not only that imitation does not always express the essential and characteristic features of the social fact, but even that it never expresses them. No doubt, every social fact is imitated; it has, as we have just shown, a tendency to become general, but that is because it is social, i.e., obligatory. Its power of expansion is not the cause but the consequence of its sociological character. If, further, only social facts produced this consequence, imitation could perhaps serve, if not to explain them, at least to define them. But an individual condition which produces a whole series of effects remains individual nevertheless. Moreover, one may ask whether the word "imitation" is indeed fitted to designate an effect due to a coercive influence. Thus, by this single expression, very different phenomena, which ought to be distinguished, are confused.

even their extent. Consequently, at the very most, it should be necessary to add to the list of phenomena which we have enumerated as presenting the distinctive criterion of a social fact only one additional category, "ways of existing"; and, as this enumeration was not meant to be rigorously exhaustive, the addition would not be absolutely necessary.

Such an addition is perhaps not necessary, for these "ways of existing" are only crystallized "ways of acting." The political structure of a society is merely the way in which its component segments have become accustomed to live with one another. If their relations are traditionally intimate, the segments tend to fuse with one another, or, in the contrary case, to retain their identity. The type of habitation imposed upon us is merely the way in which our contemporaries and our ancestors have been accustomed to construct their houses. The methods of communication are merely the channels which the regular currents of commerce and migrations have dug, by flowing in the same direction. To be sure, if the phenomena of a structural character alone presented this permanence, one might believe that they constituted a distinct species. A legal regulation is an arrangement no less permanent than a type of architecture, and yet the regulation is a "physiological" fact. A simple moral maxim is assuredly somewhat more malleable, but it is much more rigid than a simple professional custom or a fashion. There is thus a whole series of degrees without a break in continuity between the facts of the most articulated structure and those free currents of social life which are not yet definitely molded. The differences between them are, therefore, only differences in the degree of consolidation they present. Both are simply life, more or less crystallized. No doubt, it may be of some advantage to reserve the term "morphological" for those social facts which concern the social substratum, but only on condition of not overlooking the fact that they are of the same nature as the others. Our definition will then include the whole relevant range of facts if we say: *A social fact is every way of acting, fixed or not, capable of exercising on the individual an external constraint;* or again, *every way of acting which is general throughout a given society, while at the same time existing in its own right independent of its individual manifestations.*[4]

[4] This close connection between life and structure, organ and function, may be easily proved in sociology because between these two extreme terms there exists a whole series of immediately observable intermediate stages which show the bond between them. Biology is not in the same favorable position. But we may well believe that the inductions on this subject made by sociology are applicable to biology and that, in organisms as well as in societies, only differences in degree exist between these two orders of facts.

CHAPTER II

RULES FOR THE OBSERVATION
OF SOCIAL FACTS

The first and most fundamental rule is: *Consider social facts as things.*

I

At the moment when a new order of phenomena becomes the subject matter of a science, these phenomena are already represented in the mind not only by rather definite perceptions but also by some kind of crudely formed concepts. Before the first rudiments of physics and chemistry appeared, men already had some notions concerning physico-chemical phenomena which transcended mere perception, such as are found, for example, mingled in all religions. The reason for this is that thought and reflection are prior to science, which merely uses them more methodically. Man cannot live in an environment without forming some ideas about it according to which he regulates his behavior. But, because these ideas are nearer to us and more within our mental reach than the realities to which they correspond, we tend naturally to substitute them for the latter and to make them the very subject of our speculations. Instead of observing, describing, and comparing things, we are content to focus our consciousness upon, to analyze, and to combine our ideas. Instead of a science concerned with realities, we produce no more than an ideological analysis. To be sure, this analysis does not necessarily exclude all observation. One may appeal to the facts in order to confirm one's hypotheses or the final conclusions to which they lead. But in this case, facts intervene only secondarily as examples or confirmatory proofs; they are not the central subject of science. Such a science therefore proceeds from ideas to things, not from things to ideas.

It is clear that this method cannot give objective results. These ideas or concepts, whatever name one gives them, are not legitimate substitutes for things. Products of everyday experience, their primary function is to put our actions in harmony with our environment; they are created by experience and for it. Now, a representation may successfully fulfil this function while theoretically false. Several centuries have elapsed since Copernicus dissipated the illusions of the senses concerning the movements of heavenly bodies; and yet we still habitually regulate our time according to these illusions. In order to evoke the reaction required by the nature of a certain stimulus, an idea need not express that nature faithfully, but need only inform us about the useful or disadvantageous qualities of the thing. Further, the ideas thus formed are only approximately correct in the general run of cases. In fact, many times they are as dangerously incorrect as they are inadequate. By elaborating such ideas in some fashion, one will therefore never arrive at a discovery of the laws of reality. On the contrary, they are like a veil drawn between the thing and ourselves, concealing them from us the more successfully as we think them more transparent.

Not only must such a science necessarily remain in a state of stagnation, but it even lacks the materials upon which it might grow. It comes into existence but to disappear, as it were, and is replaced by art. Its concepts are supposed to contain all that is essential in reality, since they are (wrongly) identified with reality itself. Therefore, they seem to have all that is necessary to enable us not only to understand what is but to prescribe what ought to be, and to describe the means of bringing it to pass. For that which is good coincides with that which is in conformity with the nature of things; that which is contrary to this nature is bad; and the means to attain the one and escape the other derive from this same nature. If, therefore, reality can be thus understood at a glance, the study of present phenomenal reality is no longer of any practical interest; and, as this interest is the justification for its study, it is henceforth without a purpose. Thus, an incentive is given to turn from the very subject of our science, namely, the present and the past, and to proceed at once to the future. Instead of seeking a comprehension of facts already acquired, it undertakes immediately to discover new ones, more in accord with the ends pursued by men. If men think they know what the essence of matter is, they immediately start to look for the philosopher's stone. This encroachment of art on science, which prevents the development of the latter, is facilitated, moreover, by the very circumstances which determine the awakening of scientific reflection. For, since it comes into being only for the purpose of satisfying vital necessities, it finds itself quite naturally oriented toward the attainment of practical results. The needs which it is called to relieve are always urgent, and consequently hasten it on to a conclusion; they demand remedies, not explanations.

This procedure conforms so closely to the natural bent of the human mind that it is to be found in the beginnings of the physical sciences. It is this point of view which characterizes alchemy rather than chemistry, astrology rather than astronomy. It is in terms of this procedure that Bacon characterizes the method employed by the scholars of his time and which he sought to reform. The ideas just mentioned are those *notiones vulgares* or *praenotiones*[1] which he points out to be the basic ideas of all sciences,[2] where they take the place of facts.[3] These *idola*, which are illusions that distort the real aspect of things, are nevertheless mistaken for the things themselves. Therefore the mind, encountering no resistance in this imaginary world and conscious of no restraint, gives itself up to boundless ambitions and comes to believe in the possibility of constructing, or rather reconstructing, the world, by virtue of its own resources exclusively and at the whim of its desires.

If such was the case with the natural sciences, it would be much more so in the history of sociology. Man already had ideas on law, morality, the family, the state, and society itself before the advent of social science, for these ideas were necessary conditions of his life. In sociology especially, these prejudices or "idols," to use Bacon's expression again, are likely to exercise undue ascendancy over the mind and to be substituted for the study of facts. Indeed, social things are actualized only through men; they are a product of human activity. They appear to be nothing but the overt manifestation of ideas perhaps innate, contained in the mind; they are nothing but the application of these ideas to the diverse circumstances involving the relations of men. The organization of the family, of contracts, of punishment, of the state, and of society appears thus to be simply the embodiment of the ideas we hold concerning society, the state, justice, etc. Consequently, these and similar facts seem to have reality

---

[1] *Novum organum*, I, 26.   [2] *Ibid.*, p. 17.   [3] *Ibid.*, p. 36.

only in and through the ideas which are their germ, and the ideas therefore become the proper subject matter of sociology.

This approach is justified by the fact that the mind, overrun, as it is, by the details of social life which invade it from all sides, does not perceive these details clearly enough to feel their reality. Unable to perceive the relationships which would properly organize these details, they give rather easily the impression of being isolated in a vacuum, of being a substance that is half-unreal and indefinitely plastic. That is why so many thinkers have seen in our social organization only artificial and more or less arbitrary combinations. But if the concrete and particular detailed forms escape us, at least we have an approximate idea of the general aspects of collective existence; and these schematic and crystallized representations are the superficial concepts which we employ in ordinary life. We cannot doubt their existence, since we perceive it simultaneously with our own. Not only are they within us, but, as they are a product of repeated experiences, they derive from repetition and from the habit resulting from it, a sort of dominance and authority. We feel their resistance when we try to shake them off. We are bound to confer the character of reality on phenomena which oppose us. All arguments thus converge to make us find the true social reality in these phenomena.

And in truth, up to the present, sociology has dealt more or less exclusively with concepts and not with things. Comte, it is true, declared that social phenomena are natural facts, subject to natural laws. He thereby implicitly recognized their character as things, for in nature there are only things. But when he passes beyond these philosophical generalities and attempts to apply his principle and develop from it the science implied in it, he too, takes ideas for the subject matter of study. It is the course of human progress that forms the chief subject of his sociology. He begins with the idea that there is a continuous evolution of the human species, consisting in an ever more complete perfection of human nature; and his problem is to discover the order of this evolution. Now, the existence of this assumed evolution can be established only by an already completed science; it cannot, then, constitute the immediate subject of research, excepting as a conception of the mind and not as a thing. And indeed, this "representation" is so completely subjective that, as a matter of fact, this progress of humanity actually cannot be said to exist at all. It is only the individual societies which are born, develop, and die that can be observed, and therefore have objective existence. If the more recent societies were merely a continuation of their predecessors, each more advanced type could be considered as a duplication of the type immediately preceding, with something added; one could then place them all in sequential order, as it were, classifying together those displaying the same degree of development; and the series thus constituted might be regarded as representative of humanity. But the facts are not so simple. A group which succeeds another is not simply a prolongation of the latter with some newly acquired characteristics; it is qualitatively different from it, having gained some properties and lost others. It constitutes a new individuality; and all these distinct individualities, being heterogeneous, cannot be juxtaposed in the same continuous series, and surely not in a single series. For the succession of societies cannot be represented as in a single plane; it resembles, rather, a tree with branches extending in divergent directions. In short, Comte identified historical development with the idea he had of it, which does not differ much from that of the layman. Viewed from a distance, history does convey well enough this serial and simple aspect, appearing as a mere succession of individuals proceeding in the same direction because they have the same human nature. Since, moreover, it seems inconceivable to these writers that social evolution could possibly be anything but the development of some human idea, it appears quite natural to define it by the idea men form about it. Now, in proceeding thus, not only does one remain in the sphere of ideology but one assigns to sociology a concept which is not even truly sociological.

Spencer rejects this concept, but only to replace it by another which has the same faulty origin. With him societies, and not humanity, become the subject matter of science. However, in the definition he gives of society at the outset, the thing itself disappears, giving way to the preconception he has of it. He postulates as a self-evident proposition that "a society is formed only when, in addition to juxtaposition, there is co-operation"—that only by this combination does the union of individuals become a society in the strict sense of the world.[4] Then, starting from the idea that co-operation is the essence of social life, he distinguishes between two classes of societies according to the nature of the co-operation prevailing in them. "There is," he says, "a spontaneous co-operation which grows up without thought during the pursuit of private ends; and there is co-operation which, consciously devised, implies distinct recognition of common ends."[5] The former he terms "industrial"; the lat-

[4] H. Spencer, *The Principles of Sociology* (New York: D. Appleton & Co.), II, 244.

[5] *Ibid.*, p. 245.

ter "military societies." This distinction is certainly the germinal idea of his sociology.

But this initial definition defines as a thing that which is merely an idea. It is presented as the expression of an immediately observable fact since the definition is formulated at the outset as an axiom. However, mere inspection does not reveal that co-operation is the core of social life. Such an affirmation would be scientifically legitimate only after all the manifestations of collective existence had been reviewed, and it had been shown that they are all various forms of co-operation. So here again a certain conception of social reality is substituted for reality itself.[6] What is thus defined is clearly not society but Spencer's idea of it. And he has no scruples in proceeding thus, because for him, also, society is and can be only the embodiment of an idea, namely, this very idea of co-operation by which he defines it.[7] It would be easy to show that, in each of the particular problems he treats, his method remains the same. Thus, although he claims to proceed empirically, the facts accumulated in his sociology seem to function principally as arguments, since they are employed to illustrate analyses of concepts rather than to describe and explain things. Actually, all the essential points of his doctrines are capable of direct deduction from his definition of society and the different forms of co-operation. For, if our only choice is between a tyrannically imposed co-operation and a free and spontaneous one, the latter is only too evidently the ideal toward which humanity does and ought to tend.

[6] A conception, moreover, subject to controversy. (See *Division du travail social*, II, 2, 4.)

[7] "Co-operation, then, is at once that which cannot exist without a society, and that for which a society exists" (*op. cit.*, II, 244).

These lay notions are to be found not only in the basic principles of the science but also constantly in the course of the arguments. In the present state of knowledge, we cannot be certain of the exact nature of the state, of sovereignty, political liberty, democracy, socialism, communism, etc. Our method should, then, require our avoidance of all use of these concepts so long as they have not been scientifically established. And yet the words which express them recur constantly in the discussions of sociologists. They are freely employed with great assurance, as though they corresponded to things well known and precisely defined, whereas they awaken in us nothing but confused ideas, a tangle of vague impressions, prejudices, and emotions. We ridicule today the strange polemics built up by the doctors of the Middle Ages upon the basis of their concept of cold, warm, humid, dry, etc.; and we do not realize that we continue to apply that same method to that very order of phenomena which, because of its extreme complexity, admits of it less than any other.

In the special branches of sociology this ideological character is even more pronounced, especially in the case of ethics. One may, indeed, say that there is not a single system of ethics which has not developed from an initial idea in which its entire development was contained implicitly. Some believe that man possesses that idea at birth. Others, on the contrary, believe that it evolves more or less slowly in the course of history. But for all empiricists as well as for rationalists, this idea is the sole true datum in ethics. As for the details of legal and moral laws, it is affirmed that they have, as it were, no existence in their own right but are merely applications of this fundamental notion to the particular circumstances of life, varied somewhat to suit the different cases. Accordingly, the subject matter of the science of ethics cannot be this system of precepts which has no reality, but must be the idea from which the precepts are derived and of which they are only diverse applications. Furthermore, all the problems ordinarily raised in ethics refer not to things but to ideas. Moralists think it necessary to determine with precision the essence of the ideas of law and ethics, and not the nature of ethics and law. They have not yet arrived at the very simple truth that, as our ideas (*représentations*) of physical things are derived from these things themselves and express them more or less exactly, so our idea of ethics must be derived from the observable manifestation of the rules that are functioning under our eyes, rules that reproduce them in systematic form. Consequently, these rules, and not our superficial idea of them, are actually the subject matter of science, just as actual physical bodies, and not the layman's idea of them, constitute the subject matter of physics. Therefore, it is only the superstructure of ethics, viz., its prolongations and echoes in the individual consciousness, that becomes the basis of the ethical systems of these writers. And this method is applied not only to the most general problems of this science but likewise to special questions. From the fundamental ethical concepts which are treated first, the moralist proceeds to the derived ideas of family, country, responsibility, charity, and justice; and it is always with ideas that his reflection is concerned.

In political economy the same situation exists. Its subject matter, says John Stuart Mill, consists of those social facts the goal of which, principally or exclusively, is the acquisition of wealth.[8] But in order to be able to relate the

[8] *System of Logic*, III, 496.

facts thus defined as things, to the observation of the scholar, it would, at the very least, be necessary to indicate by what criteria the facts satisfying this condition are to be recognized. Now, when a science is in its infancy, we do not have the right to affirm the existence of such facts, to say nothing of asserting the possibility of their identification. Indeed, in every branch of research, it is possible to establish that facts have a meaning, and what the meaning is, only when the explanation of the facts is sufficiently advanced. There is no problem more complex or less likely to be solved on the first attempt. Nothing, then, assures us in advance of the existence of a sphere of social activity wherein the desire for wealth really plays such a preponderant role. Consequently, the subject matter of economics, so defined, comprises not the realities given to immediate observation but merely conjectures that are the product of pure intellect. They are "facts" imagined by the economist as being related to the above-mentioned end, and they are facts to the extent that he recognizes them as facts. For example, when he undertakes the study of what he calls "production," he thinks he can straightway enumerate and review the principal agents of that process. He does not, then, determine them by observing the conditions upon which the thing he was studying depends, for then he would have begun by a description of his observations from which he drew his conclusion. If, from the beginning of his research and in a few words, he proceeds to this classification, it is because he has obtained it by a simple, logical analysis. He starts from the idea of production; in analyzing it, he finds that it implies logically the ideas of natural forces, of work, and of tools or capital, and he likewise treats in their turn these derivative ideas.[9]

The most fundamental of all economic theories, that of value, is manifestly constructed according to this same method. If value had been studied as any fact of reality ought to be studied, the economist would indicate, first of all, by what characteristics one might recognize the thing so designated, then classify its varieties, investigate by methodical inductions what the causes of its variations are, and finally compare these various results in order to abstract a general formula. Theory would be introduced only when science had reached a sufficient stage of advancement. On the contrary, it is introduced at the very outset. In order to construct economic theory, the economist is content to meditate and to focus his attention on his own idea of value, that is, as an object capable of being exchanged; he finds therein the idea of utility, scarcity, etc., and with these products of his analysis he constructs his definition. To be sure, he confirms it by several examples. But, considering the innumerable facts such a theory must account for, how can one grant even the slightest validity to the necessarily limited number of facts thus cited at random?

Thus, the actual contribution of scientific investigation to economics and ethics is very limited, while that of art is preponderant. Ethical theory is limited merely to a few discussions on the idea of duty, the good and right. And even these abstract speculations do not constitute a science,

[9] The ideological nature of economics is implied even in the expressions used by economists. The question is always one of the concept of utility, savings, investment, expenditure. (See Gide, *Principes d'économie politique*, Book III, chap. i, § i; chap. ii, § i; chap. iii, § i.)

strictly speaking, since their object is the determination not of that which is, in fact, the supreme rule of morality but of what it ought to be. Similarly, economists are today principally occupied with the problem of whether society *ought to* be organized on an individualistic or socialistic basis, whether it is *better* that the state should intervene in industrial and commercial relations, or whether it is *better* to abandon them to private initiative; whether one ought to use a single monetary standard, or a bimetallic system, etc. It contains few laws in the proper sense of the word; even what are commonly called "laws" are generally unworthy of this designation since they are merely maxims for action, or practical precepts in disguise. The famous law of supply and demand, for example, has never been inductively established, as should be the case with a law referring to economic reality. No experiment or systematic comparison has ever been undertaken for the purpose of establishing that, *in fact*, economic relations *do* conform to this law. All that these economists could do, and actually did do, was to demonstrate by dialectics that, in order properly to promote their interests, individuals ought to proceed according to this law, and that every other line of action would be harmful to those who engage in it and would imply a serious error of judgment. It is fair and logical that the most productive industries should be the most attractive and that the holders of the products most in demand and most scarce should sell them at the highest prices. But this quite logical necessity resembles in no way the necessity that the true laws of nature present. The latter express the regulations according to which facts are really interconnected, not the way in which it is good that they should be interconnected.

What we say of this law may be repeated for all those that

orthodox economics designates as "natural" and which, moreover, are scarcely more than particular cases of it. They are natural, if one likes, in the sense that they enunciate the means which it is really or seemingly natural to employ in order to attain a certain hypothetical end, but they do not deserve this designation if natural law means an inductively determined way of behavior in nature. In brief, they are merely maxims of practical wisdom; and they have been more or less plausibly presented as the very expression of reality only because it was supposed, rightly or wrongly, that these counsels were indeed followed by the average man in the average case.

In spite of all these doctrines, social phenomena are things and ought to be treated as things. To demonstrate this proposition, it is unnecessary to philosophize on their nature and to discuss the analogies they present with the phenomena of lower realms of existence. It is sufficient to note that they are the unique data of the sociologist. All that is given, all that is subject to observation, has thereby the character of a thing. To treat phenomena as things is to treat them as data, and these constitute the point of departure of science. Now, social phenomena present this character incontestably. What is given is not the idea that men form of value, for that is inaccessible, but only the values established in the course of economic relations; not conceptions of the moral ideal, but the totality of rules which actually determine conduct; not the idea of utility or wealth, but all the details of economic organization. Even assuming the possibility that social life is merely the development of certain ideas, these ideas are nevertheless not immediately given. They cannot be perceived or known directly, but only through the phenomenal reality expressing them. We do not know a priori whether ideas form the basis of the diverse currents of social life, nor what they are. Only after having traced these currents back to their sources shall we know whence they issue.

We must, therefore, consider social phenomena in themselves as distinct from the consciously formed representations of them in the mind; we must study them objectively as external things, for it is this character that they present to us. If this exteriority should prove to be only apparent, the advance of science will bring the disillusionment and we shall see our conception of social phenomena change, as it were, from the objective to the subjective. But in any case, the solution cannot be anticipated; and even if we finally arrive at the result that social phenomena do not possess all the intrinsic characteristics of the thing, we ought at first to treat them as if they had. This rule is applicable, then, to all social reality without exception. Even phenomena which give the strongest impression of being arbitrary arrangements ought to be thus considered. *The voluntary character of a practice or an institution should never be assumed beforehand.* Moreover, if we may introduce our personal observation, it has always been our experience that, when this procedure is followed, facts most arbitrary in appearance will come to present, after more attentive observation, qualities of consistency and regularity that are symptomatic of their objectivity.

The foregoing statements concerning the distinctive characteristics of the social fact give us sufficient assurance about the nature of this objectivity to prove that it is not illusory. Indeed, the most important characteristic of a "thing" is the impossibility of its modification by a simple effort of the will. Not that the thing is refractory to all modification, but a mere act of the will is insufficient to produce a change in it; it requires a more or less strenuous effort due to the resistance which it offers, and, moreover, the effort is not always successful. We have already seen that social facts have this characteristic. Far from being a product of the will, they determine it from without; they are like molds in which our actions are inevitably shaped. This necessity is often inescapable. But even when we triumph over it, the opposition encountered signifies clearly to us the presence of something not depending upon ourselves. Thus, in considering social phenomena as things, we merely adjust our conceptions in conformity to their nature.

Clearly, the reform needed in sociology is at all points identical with that which has transformed psychology in the last thirty years. Just as Comte and Spencer declare that social facts are facts of nature, without, however, treating them as things, so the different empirical schools had long recognized the natural character of psychological phenomena, but continued to apply to them a purely ideological method. In fact, the empiricists, not less than their adversaries, proceeded exclusively by introspection. Now, the facts obtained thereby are too few in number, too fleeting and plastic, to be able to control and to correct the corresponding ideas fixed in us by habit. If they are not subjected to some other check, nothing counterbalances them; consequently, they take the place of facts and become the subject matter of science. Thus, neither Locke nor Condillac studied psychological phenomena objectively. They did not study sensation in itself but their particular idea of it. Therefore, although in certain respects they prepared the way for scientific psychology, its actual origin is to be dated much later, when it had finally been established that states of consciousness can and ought to be considered from without, and not from the point of view of the consciousness experiencing them. Such is the great revolution accomplished in this branch of studies. All the specific procedures and all the new methods by which this science has been enriched are only diverse means of realizing more completely this fundamental idea. It remains for sociology to make this same advance, to pass from the subjective stage, which it has still scarcely outgrown, to the objective.

Fortunately, this transformation is less difficult to effect here than in psychology. Indeed, psychological facts are naturally given as conscious states of the individual, from whom they do not seem to be even separable. Internal by definition, it seems that they can be treated as external only by doing violence to their nature. Not only is an effort of abstraction necessary, but in addition a whole series of procedures and artifices in order to hold them continuously within this point of view. Social facts, on the contrary, qualify far more naturally and immediately as things. Law is embodied in codes; the currents of daily life are recorded in statistical figures and historical monuments; fashions are preserved in costumes; and taste in works of art. By their very nature they tend toward an independent existence outside the individual consciousnesses, which they dominate. In order to disclose their character as things, it is unnecessary to manipulate them ingeniously. From this point of view, sociology has a significant advantage over psychology, an advantage not hitherto perceived, and one which should hasten its development. Its facts are perhaps more difficult to interpret because more complex, but they are more easily arrived at. Psychology, on the contrary, has difficulties not only in the manipulation of its facts but also in rendering them explicit. Consequently, we believe that, once this principle of sociological method is generally recognized and practiced, sociology will progress with a rapidity difficult to forecast from its present tardiness of development and will even overtake psychology, whose present relative advantage is due solely to historical priority.[10]

II

But the experience of our predecessors has shown that, in order to assure the practical realization of the truth just enunciated, it is not enough to be thoroughly convinced one's self, or even to set forth a theoretical demonstration of it. The mind is so naturally inclined to underrate and disregard this particular truth that a relapse into the old errors will inevitably follow unless sociologists are willing to submit themselves to a rigorous discipline. We shall therefore formulate the principal rules for such a discipline, all of them corollaries of the foregoing theorem.

1. The first corollary is: *All preconceptions must be eradicated.* A special demonstration of this rule is unnecessary; it follows easily from all our previous statements. It is, moreover, the basis of all scientific method. The logical doubt of Descartes is, in its essence, only an application of it. If, at the moment of the foundation of science, Descartes resolves to question all ideas he had previously received, it is because he wishes to employ only scientifically developed concepts, that is, concepts constructed according to the method instituted by himself; all those having some other origin, then,

[10] It is true that the greater complexity of social facts makes the science more difficult. But, in compensation, precisely because sociology is the latest comer, it is in a position to profit by the progress made in the sciences concerned with lower stages of existence and to learn from them. This utilization of previous experiments will certainly accelerate its development.

must be rejected, at least provisionally. We have already seen that Bacon's theory of the "idols" has the same meaning. The two great doctrines that have been so often opposed to one another thus agree on this essential point. The sociologist ought, therefore, whether at the moment of the determination of his research objectives or in the course of his demonstrations, to repudiate resolutely the use of concepts orginating outside of science for totally unscientific needs. He must emancipate himself from the fallacious ideas that dominate the mind of the layman; he must throw off, once and for all, the yoke of these empirical categories, which from long continued habit have become tyrannical. At the very least, if at times he is obliged to resort to them, he ought to do so fully conscious of their trifling value, so that he will not assign to them a role out of proportion to their real importance.

The frequent interference of sentiment makes this emancipation from lay ideas particularly difficult in sociology. Indeed, our political and religious beliefs and our moral standards carry with them an emotional tone that is not characteristic of our attitude toward physical objects; consequently, this emotional character infects our manner of conceiving and explaining them. The ideas we form of things have a vital interest for us, just as the objects, themselves, and thus assume an authority which brooks no contradiction. Every opinion that disturbs them is treated with hostility. If a proposition is not in agreement, for example, with one's idea of patriotism or of individual dignity, it is denied, whatever its proofs may be. We cannot admit its truth; it is given no consideration at all; and our emotion, to justify our attitude, has no difficulty in suggesting reasons that are readily found convincing. These ideas may, indeed, have such prestige that they do not even tolerate scientific examination. The very fact of submitting them, as well as the phenomena they represent, to cold, dry analysis, is revolting to certain minds. Whoever undertakes the study of morality objectively, and as an external reality, seems to these sensitive creatures to be devoid of all moral sense, just as the vivisectionist seems to the layman devoid of common sensibility. Far from admitting that these sentiments should themselves be drawn under scientific scrutiny, it is to them that these writers feel they must appeal in order to treat scientifically the parallel social facts.

"Woe to the scholar," writes an eloquent historian of religions, "who approaches divine matters without having in the depths of his consciousness, in the innermost indestructible regions of his being, where the souls of his ancestors sleep, an unknown sanctuary from which rises now and then the aroma of incense, a line of a psalm, a sorrowful or triumphal cry that as a child he sent to heaven along with his brothers, and that creates immediate communion with the prophets of yore!"[11]

One cannot protest too strongly against this mystical doctrine, which, like all mysticism, is essentially a disguised empiricism, the negation of all science. Sentiments pertaining to social things enjoy no privilege not possessed by other sentiments, for their origin is the same. They, too, have been formed in the course of history; they are a product of human experience, which is, however, confused and unorganized. They are not due to some transcendental insight into reality but result from all sorts of impressions and emotions accumulated according to circumstances, without order and without methodical interpretation. Far from conveying in-

[11] J. Darmesteter, *Les Prophètes d'Israël*, p. 9.

sights superior to rational ones, these sentiments are simply strong but confused states of mind. To accord them a dominant role means giving supremacy to the inferior faculties of intelligence over the superior, condemning one's self to pure logomachy. Such a science can satisfy only those who prefer to think with their feelings and emotions rather than with their understanding, and who prefer the immediate and confused syntheses of first impression to the patient and luminous analyses of reason. Sentiment is a subject for scientific study, not the criterion of scientific truth. Moreover, every science encounters analogous resistances at the outset. There was a time when sentiments relating to the things of the physical world opposed with equal energy the establishment of the physical sciences, because they, too, had a religious or moral character. We believe, therefore, that this prejudice, pursued from one science to the next, will finally disappear also from its last retreat, sociology, leaving a free field for the true scientific endeavor.

2. As it happens, this first rule for sociology is entirely negative. It teaches the sociologist to escape the realm of lay ideas and to turn his attention toward facts, but it does not tell him how to take hold of the facts in order to study them objectively.

Every scientific investigation is directed toward a limited class of phenomena, included in the same definition. The first step of the sociologist, then, ought to be to define the things he treats, in order that his subject matter may be known. This is the first and most indispensable condition of all proofs and verifications. A theory, indeed, can be checked only if we know how to recognize the facts of which it is intended to give an account. Moreover, since this initial definition determines the very subject matter of science, this subject matter will or will not be a thing, depending on the nature of the definition.

In order to be objective, the definition must obviously deal with phenomena not as ideas but in terms of their inherent properties. It must characterize them by elements essential to their nature, not by their conformity to an intellectual ideal. Now, at the very beginning of research, when the facts have not yet been analyzed, the only ascertainable characteristics are those external enough to be immediately perceived. Those that are less obvious may be perhaps more significant, and their explanatory value is more important; but they are unknown to science at this stage, and they can be anticipated only by substituting some hypothetical conception in the place of reality. It is imperative, then, that the material included under this fundamental definition be sought among the more external characteristics of sociological phenomena. On the other hand, this definition should include, without exception or distinction, all phenomena presenting to an equal extent these characteristics, for we have neither the reason nor the means for choosing among them. These characteristics are our only clue to reality; consequently, they must be given complete authority in our selection of facts. No other criterion could even partially justify any suspension of, or exception to, this rule. Whence our second corollary: *The subject matter of every sociological study should comprise a group of phenomena defined in advance by certain common external characteristics, and all phenomena so defined should be included within this group.*

For example, we note the existence of certain acts, all presenting the external characteristic that they evoke from society the particular reaction called punishment. We constitute them as a separate group, to which we give a common label; we call every punished act a crime, and crime thus defined becomes the object of a special science, criminology. Similarly, we observe within all known societies small groups whose special characteristic is that they are composed preponderantly of individuals who are blood-kin, united by legal bonds. We classify together the facts relating thereto, and give a particular name to the group of facts so created, "domestic relations." We call every aggregate of this kind a family, and this becomes the subject of a special investigation which has not yet received a specific name in sociological terminology. In passing from the family in general to the different family types, the same rule should be applied. For example, the study of the clan and the matriarchal or the patriarchal family should begin with a definition constructed according to the same method. The field of each problem, whether general or particular, must be similarly circumscribed.

By proceeding thus, the sociologist, from the very first, is firmly grounded in reality. Indeed, the pattern of such a classification does not depend on him or on the cast of his individual mind but on the nature of things. The criteria according to which they are placed in a particular category can be recognized by everyone; and the concepts thus formed do not always, or even generally, tally with that of the layman. For example, manfestations of free thought or violations of etiquette, so regularly and severely penalized in many societies, are evidently considered crimes in the common-sense view even in these societies. Similarly, in the usual acceptance of the words a clan is not a family. But such discrepancies are not important, for it is not our aim simply to discover a method for identifying with sufficient accuracy the facts to which the words of ordinary language refer and the ideas they convey. We need, rather, to formulate entirely new concepts, appropriate to the requirements of science and expressed in an appropriate terminology. Of course, lay concepts are not entirely useless to the scholar; they serve as suggestions and guides. They inform us of the existence, somewhere, of an aggregation of phenomena which, bearing the same name, must, in consequence, probably have certain characteristics in common. Since these concepts have always had some reference to phenomena, they even indicate to us at times, though roughly, where these phenomena are to be found. But, as they have been crudely formed, they quite naturally do not coincide exactly with the scientific concepts, which have been established for a set purpose.[12]

This rule, as obvious and important as it is, is seldom observed in sociology. Precisely because it treats everyday things, such as the family, property, crime, etc., the sociologist most often thinks it unnecessary to define them rigorously at the outset. We are so accustomed to use these terms, and they recur so constantly in our conversation, that it seems unnecessary to render their meaning precise. We simply refer to the common notion, but this common notion is very often ambiguous. As a result of this ambiguity, things that are very different in reality are given the same

[12] In actual practice one always starts with the lay concept and the lay term. One inquires whether, among the things which this word confusedly connotes, there are some which present common external characteristics. If this is the case, and if the concept formed by the grouping of the facts thus brought together coincides, if not totally (which is rare), at least to a large extent, with the lay concept, it will be possible to continue to designate the former by the same term as the latter, that is, to retain in science the expression used in everyday language. But if the gap is too considerable, if the common notion confuses a plurality of distinct ideas, the creation of new and distinctive terms becomes necessary.

name and the same explanation, and this leads to boundless confusion.

For example, two sorts of monogamous unions exist: those monogamous in fact, and those monogamous by law. In the former, the husband has only one wife, although he is allowed by law to possess several; in the latter, polygamy is legally forbidden. In several animal species and in certain primitive societies monogamy "in fact" is to be found, not sporadically, but with the same prevalence as if imposed by law. When a tribe is dispersed over a vast area, there is little social contact, and consequently the individuals live isolated from one another. In such a case each man naturally seeks only one wife, because in this state of isolation it is difficult for him to secure several. Compulsory monogamy, on the contrary, is observed only in the highest societies. These two types of conjugal unions have, then, a very different significance; and yet the same word serves to designate them both. We commonly call certain animals "monogamous," although they have nothing resembling legal control. Now Spencer, in his study of marriage, uses the word "monogamy" in its ordinary equivocal meaning, without defining it. As a result the evolution of marriage seems to him to present an unaccountable anomaly, since he thinks he observes a higher form of the sexual union as early as the first phases of historical development, while it seems to disappear in the intermediate period, only to reappear later. He then concludes that there is no positive correlation between social progress in general and progress toward a perfect type of family life. A timely definition would have prevented this error.[13]

[13] The same absence of definition caused the occasional statements that democracy is realized both at the beginning and at the end of history. The truth is that primitive and modern democracy are very different from one another.

In other cases great care may be exercised in defining the objects of investigation; but instead of grouping under the same heading all phenomena having the same external properties, only a selected number of them are included. Thus, only certain ones are designated as a kind of "élite," and these alone are regarded as coming within the category. As for the others, they are considered as having usurped these distinctive signs and are disregarded. It is easy to foresee that in this way only a subjective and incomplete picture can be attained. Such an omission can be made only by applying a preconceived idea, since, at the beginning of science, no research could possibly have already established the legitimacy of this usurpation, even if it were possible to have done so. The only possible reason for retaining the phenomena chosen was, then, that they conformed, more than the others, to a certain ideal conception concerning this sort of reality.

For example, M. Garofalo, at the beginning of his *Criminologie*, demonstrates very well that "the sociological concept of crime"[14] has to form the point of departure of this science. Only, in setting up his concept, he does not compare indiscriminately all acts which have been repressed by regular punishments in the different social types. He compares only certain ones among them, namely, those offending the most general and universal of the moral feelings. The moral sentiments which have disappeared in the course of evolution are not, to him, grounded in the nature of things, since they have not survived; consequently, the acts which have been deemed criminal because of their violation of these particular sentiments seem to him to have owed this designation only to accidental and more or less pathological circumstances. But it is by virtue of an entirely personal

[14] *Op. cit.*, p. 2.

conception of morality that he makes this elimination. He starts from the idea that moral evolution, taken at its very fount or near its source, carries with it all sorts of dross and impurities, which it then progressively eliminates, and that it is only today that it has succeeded in freeing itself from all the adventitious elements which, in primitive times, troubled its course. But this principle is neither an evident axiom nor a demonstrated truth; it is only a hypothesis, and indeed one without justification. The variable aspects of the moral sense are not less grounded in the nature of things than are the immutable; the variations in standards of morality merely testify to the corresponding variations in life. In zoölogy, the forms peculiar to the lower species are not regarded as less natural than those occurring at the other points on the evolutionary scale. Similarly, these acts which were condemned as crimes by primitive societies and have since lost this designation are really criminal in relation to these societies, quite like those which we continue to repress today. The former correspond to the changing, the latter to the constant, conditions of social life; but the former are not any more artificial than those acts which are considered crimes today.

But, even if these acts had unduly assumed the criminal character, they ought not to be sharply separated from the others; for the pathological forms of a phenomenon are not different in nature from the normal forms, and it is therefore necessary to observe the former as well as the latter in order to determine this nature. Morbidity is not absolutely anti-thetical to health; these are two varieties of the same phenomenon, and each tends to explain the other. This is a rule long recognized and practiced in biology and in psychology, and the sociologist is equally under an obligation to respect it. Unless one asserts that the same phenomenon can be due sometimes to one cause and sometimes to another, that is, unless one denies the principle of causality, the causes which impress on an act the mark of crime, in an abnormal manner, cannot differ qualitatively from those producing the same effect in a normal manner; they differ only in degree or they differ because they do not act in the same environment. The abnormal crime, then, is still a crime and ought, consequently, to be included in the definition of crime. What M. Garofalo actually does is to take as the genus that which is only a species or merely a simple variety. The facts to which his definition of criminality applies represent only an infinitesimal minority among those it should include, for it applies neither to religious crimes, nor to violations of etiquette, ceremonial, tradition, etc. If these have disappeared from our modern codes, they make up, on the contrary, almost the entire penal law of former societies.

The same flaw in method causes certain observers to deny the existence of any species of morality among savages.[15] They start with the idea that our morality is *the* morality. It is evident, however, that our morality is either unknown or in a rudimentary state among primitive peoples and that this discrimination is clearly arbitrary. If we apply our second corollary in this case, everything changes. To decide whether a precept belongs to the moral order, we must determine whether or not it presents the external mark of morality; this mark is a widespread repressive sanction, that is, a condemnation by public opinion that punishes all violations of the precept. Whenever we are presented with

---

[15] See Lubbock, *Origin of Civilization*, chap. viii: It is a still more widespread, and not less false, opinion that the ancient religions are amoral or immoral. The truth is that they have a morality of their own.

a fact having this characteristic, we have no right to deny its moral character, for this characteristic proves that it has the same nature as other moral facts. Not only are social regulations of this kind met with in primitive societies, but they are even more numerous there than in civilized societies. A large number of acts which today are left to the free choice of individuals are obligatory among them. Thus we may realize the errors we commit by omitting definitions or by defining inadequately.

But, it will be said that, in defining phenomena by their apparent characteristics, we are allowing to certain superficial properties a significance greater than that of more fundamental attributes. Are we not, by a veritable inversion of logical order, beginning at the summit instead of the base? Thus, when we define crime in terms of punishment, one is almost inevitably exposed to the accusation of deriving crime from punishment, or, as a well-known quotation puts it, of considering the scaffold, and not the crime, as the source of ignominy. This reproach rests upon a confusion. Since the definition in question is placed at the beginnings of the science, it cannot possibly aim at a statement concerning the essence of reality; that must be attained subsequently. The sole function of the definition is to establish contact with things; and since the latter can be grasped by the mind only from its exteriors, the definition expresses them in terms of their external qualities. It does not explain these things thereby; it furnishes merely a just basis for further explanations. Certainly, punishment is not the essence of crime; but it does constitute a symptom thereof, and consequently, in order to understand crime, we must begin with punishment.

The aforementioned objection would be well founded only

if these external characteristics were at the same time accidental, that is, if they were not bound up with the fundamental properties of things. Under these conditions indeed, after science had pointed them out, it could not possibly go farther; it could not penetrate the deeper layers of reality, since there would be no necessary connection between surface and essence. But, if the principle of causality is valid, when certain characteristics are found identically and without exceptions in all the phenomena of a certain order, one may be assured that they are closely connected with the nature of the latter and bound up with it. And if to a given group of acts there is attached also the peculiarity of a penal sanction, an intimate bond must exist between punishment and the intrinsic attributes of these acts. Consequently, however superficial they may be, these properties, provided that they have been systematically observed, clearly point out to the scientist the course which he must follow in order to penetrate more to the core of the things in question. They are the first and indispensable link in the sequence to be unfolded by science in the course of its explanations.

Since objects are perceived only through sense perception, we can conclude: Science, to be objective, ought to start, not with concepts formed independent to them, but with these same perceptions. It ought to borrow the materials for its initial definitions directly from perceptual data. And, as a matter of fact, one need only reflect on the real nature of scientific work to understand that it cannot proceed otherwise. It needs concepts that adequately express things as they actually are, and not as everyday life finds it useful to conceive them. Now those concepts formulated without the discipline of science do not fulfil this condition. Science, then, has to create new concepts; it must dismiss all lay notions and the terms expressing them, and return to sense perception, the primary and necessary substance underlying all concepts. From sensation all general ideas flow, whether they be true or false, scientific or impressionistic. The point of departure of science, or speculative knowledge, cannot be different from that of lay, or practical, knowledge. It is only beyond this point, namely, in the manner of elaboration of these common data, that divergences begin.

3. But sensation may easily be subjective. It is a rule in the natural sciences to discard those data of sensation that are too subjective, in order to retain exclusively those presenting a sufficient degree of objectivity. Thus the physicist substitutes, for the vague impressions of temperature and electricity, the visual registrations of the thermometer or the electrometer. The sociologist must take the same precautions. The external characteristics in terms of which he defines the objects of his researches should be as objective as possible.

We may lay down as a principle that social facts lend themselves more readily to objective representation in proportion as their separation from the individual facts expressing them is more complete. Indeed, the degree of objectivity of a sense perception is proportionate to the degree of stability of its object; for objectivity depends upon the existence of a constant and identical point of reference to which the representation can be referred and which permits the elimination of what is variable, and hence subjective, in it. But if the points of reference themselves are variable, if they are perpetually shifting in relation to each other, there is no common standard, and the scientist has no means of distinguishing between those impressions which are external and those that are subjective. So long as social life is not separated from the individual or particular events which comprise it, and has no separate existence, it will present this dilemma. As these events differ among themselves and change in time, and as we assume the life of society to be inseparable from them, they communicate their mutability to it. Social life consists, then, of free currents perpetually in the process of transformation and incapable of being mentally fixed by the observer, and the scholar cannot approach the study of social reality from this angle. But we know that it possesses the power of crystallization without ceasing to be itself. Thus, apart from the individual acts to which they give rise, collective habits find expression in definite forms: legal rules, moral regulations, popular proverbs, social conventions, etc. As these forms have a permanent existence and do not change with the diverse applications made of them, they constitute a fixed object, a constant standard within the observer's reach, exclusive of subjective impressions and purely personal observations. A legal regulation is what it is, and there are no two ways of looking at it. Since, on the other hand, these practices are merely social life consolidated, it is legitimate, except where otherwise stated,[16] to study the latter through the former.

When, then, the sociologist undertakes the investigation of some order of social facts, he must endeavor to consider them from an aspect that is independent of their individual manifestations. It is this principle that we have applied in studying the diverse forms of social solidarity and their evolution, through the medium of the legal structure which reflects

[16] It would be necessary, for example, in order to invalidate this substitution, to have reason to believe that, at a given moment, law no longer expresses the actual state of social relations.

them.[17] On the other hand, an attempt to distinguish and classify the different family types on the basis of the literary description given us by travelers and historians is exposed to the danger of confusing the most diverse species and of bringing together the most dissimilar types. If the legal structure of the family and, more specifically, the right of succession are taken as the basis of classification, objective criteria are at hand which, while not infallible, will prevent many errors.[18] In order to classify the different kinds of crimes, one has to try to reconstruct the ways of living and the occupational customs that are practiced in the different worlds of crime. One will then recognize as many criminological types as there are different forms of this organization. To achieve an understanding of customs and popular beliefs, one must investigate the proverbs and epigrams that express them. No doubt, in proceeding thus, we leave the concrete data of collective life temporarily outside the realm of science; and yet, however changeable and unstable it may be, its unintelligibility need not be assumed. In order to follow a methodical course, we must establish the foundations of science on solid ground and not on shifting sand. We must approach the social realm where it offers the easiest access to scientific investigation. Only subsequently will it be possible to push research further and, by successive approximations, to encompass, little by little, this fleeting reality, which the human mind will never, perhaps, be able to grasp completely.

[17] See *Division du travail social*, Book I.

[18] Cf. the author's "Introduction à la sociologie de la famille," in *Annales de la Faculté des lettres de Bordeaux, 1889.*

CHAPTER III

RULES FOR DISTINGUISHING BETWEEN THE NORMAL AND THE PATHOLOGICAL

Observation conducted according to the preceding rules covers two types of facts which are very dissimilar in certain respects: those which conform to given standards and those which "ought" to be different—in other words, normal and pathological phenomena. We have seen that it is necessary to include them both in the definition with which all research must begin. But if their nature is in certain respects identical, they constitute, nevertheless, two different varieties of facts, which need to be distinguished. Can science make this distinction?

The question is of the greatest importance, for on its solution depends the role assigned to science, and especially to the science of man. According to a theory whose partisans belong to most diverse schools, science can teach us nothing about what we ought to desire. It is concerned, they say, only with facts which all have the same value and interest for us; it observes and explains, but does not judge them. Good and evil do not exist for science. It can, indeed, tell us how given causes produce their effects, but not what ends should be pursued. In order to determine not what is but what is desirable, we need to resort to the unconscious, by whatever name it may be designated: "feeling," "instinct," "vital urge," etc. Science, says a writer already quoted, can indeed illuminate the world, but it leaves darkness in our hearts; the heart must find its own light. Science thus loses all, or almost all, practical effectiveness and, consequently, its principal justification for existence. Why strive for knowledge of reality if this knowledge cannot serve us in life? To this we can make reply that, by revealing the causes of phenomena, science furnishes the means of producing them. Every means is from another point of view, an end. In order to put it into operation, it must be willed quite as much as the end whose realization it prepares. There are always several routes that lead to a given goal; a choice must therefore be made between them. If science cannot indicate the best goal to us, how can it inform us about the best means to reach it? Why should it recommend the most rapid in preference to the most economical, the surest rather than the simplest, or vice versa? If science cannot guide us in the determination of ultimate ends, it is equally powerless in the case of those secondary and subordinate ends called "means."

It is true that the ideological method offers an escape from this mysticism, and it is perhaps this circumstance which has made for the persistence of this method. Its adherents were, indeed, too much inclined to rationalism to deny that human conduct needed to be directed by reflection; but, so long as they considered phenomena independently of all subjective data, they could not find a criterion which would permit their classification according to practical value. It seemed, then, that the only means of judging them in this respect was to relate them to some master-concept; and from this argument the use of a concept governing the collation of facts, instead of being derived from them, became indispensable to all rational sociology. We must realize, however, that if, under these conditions, applied science becomes reflective, reflection thus employed is certainly not scientific.

It is yet possible for us to vindicate the legitimate rights of reason in the solution of the problem just stated, without reverting to ideology. Briefly, for societies as for individuals, health is good and desirable; disease, on the contrary, is bad and to be avoided. If, then, we can find an objective criterion, inherent in the facts themselves, which enables us to distinguish scientifically between health and morbidity in the various orders of social phenomena, science will be in a position to throw light on practical problems and still remain faithful to its own method.

Since it cannot at present arrive at formulations concerning the individual, it can give us general indications, which may in turn be appropriately modified by direct contact with the individual through sensation. The state of health, as defined by science, cannot fit exactly any individual subject, since it can be established only with relation to average circumstances, from which everyone deviates more or less; nevertheless, it may serve as a valuable point of reference for regulating our conduct. The necessity for adjusting this standard to each individual case does not mean that knowledge of it is useless. Quite the contrary, it constitutes the norm on which all our practical reasoning has to be based. Under these conditions we are no longer justified in saying that thought is of no use to action. There is no longer a gulf between science and art; but on the contrary, there is break of continuity between them. Science, it is true, can only attain facts through art, but art is merely the prolongation of science. Moreover, may it not be assumed that the practical insufficiency of the latter will diminish when the laws established by it express more and more completely individual reality?

I

Pain is commonly regarded by the layman as the index of morbidity; and in general it is true that there is a relation between these two conditions, but a relation which lacks uniformity and precision. There are serious but painless maladies; while less serious afflictions, such as those resulting from a speck of coal dust in the eye, may cause real torture. In certain cases the very absence of pain, or even actual pleasure, are symptoms of morbidity. There is an insensibility to pain which is pathological. Circumstances causing suffering to a healthy man may give to a neurasthenic a sensation of enjoyment of an incontestably morbid nature. Conversely, pain accompanies many states belonging to normal physiology, such as hunger, fatigue, and parturition.

Shall we say that health, consisting in successful development of the vital forces, is recognizable by the perfect adaptation of the organism to its environment; and shall we, on the contrary, term "morbidity" whatever disturbs this adaptation? But first—and we shall return to this point later—it has by no means been proved that every state of the organism corresponds to some external state of the environment. And, further, even if this criterion of adaptation were truly distinctive of the state of health, another criterion would be needed in order to recognize it. We must be able to distinguish varying degrees of completeness of adaptation.

Or shall we take as this criterion the effect health and morbidity may have on our probabilities of survival? Health would then be the state of an organism in which these probabilities are at a maximum; and morbidity, on the contrary, would include everything which reduces them. Unquestionably, morbidity weakens the organism. But it is not alone in producing this result. The functions of reproduction inevitably cause death in certain lower species, and they are accompanied by risks even in the higher orders. They are, however, normal. Senility and infancy have the same effects, for both the old and the very young are peculiarly susceptible to the causes of destruction. Are infancy and old age morbid types then? And can only the adult be healthy? How strangely would the domain of health and physiology then be˙restricted!

If, moreover, old age is already synonymous with morbidity, how distinguish the healthy from the diseased old person? From the same point of view, one is obliged to place menstruation among the morbid phenomena, for the disturbances it causes increase female susceptibility to disease. But would we then be justified in designating as "morbid" a state whose absence or premature disappearance constitutes an incontestably pathological phenomenon? People argue about this question as if, in a healthy organism, each element played a useful role, as if each internal state corresponded exactly to some external condition and, consequently, helped to maintain vital equilibrium and to diminish the chance of death. But it is, on the contrary, legitimate to suppose that some anatomical or functional arrangements are of no direct use, but are merely the products of the general conditions of life. We cannot, however, call them morbid, for morbidity is, above all, something escapable, something not essential to the constitution of the organism. It may even be true that, instead of strengthening the organism, these anatomical and functional arrangements diminish its resistance and, consequently, increase the risks of death.

Moreover, it is not certain that morbidity always has the consequences by which it is proposed to define it. Are there not many ailments too trivial to have an appreciable effect on the fundamental health of the organism? Even among the more serious, there are some whose consequences are not at all harmful, if we know how to combat them. The dyspeptic who follows a good hygienic routine can live to be as old as the healthy man. He is, no doubt, compelled to take certain precautions; but is this not true of us all? Can life be maintained otherwise? Each one of us has his appropriate regimen; that of the sick man does not resemble that practiced by the man who is the average of his time and environment; but this is the only difference between them. Disease does not always leave us helpless or in a state of irremediable maladaptation; it only constrains us to adapt ourselves differently from most of our fellows. There may even exist maladies which will eventually prove useful. The smallpox with which we inoculate ourselves by vaccine is a real disease that we voluntarily undergo, and yet it increases our chances of survival. There are perhaps many other cases in which the disturbance caused by the malady is insignificant compared with the immunities it confers.

Finally and above all, this criterion is most often practically inapplicable. The most we can do is to establish that the lowest mortality-rate known occurs in a specified group of individuals; the impossibility of still lower rates cannot be proved. How do we know that other conditions would not reduce the mortality-rate still further? This actual minimum is not, then, a proof of perfect adaptation, nor, therefore, a sure index of the state of health, if we adhere to the preceding definition. Further, a group exhibiting this characteristic would be very difficult to establish and to isolate— yet this would be necessary in order to discover the organic constitution peculiar to it and the supposed cause of its superiority. And while, in the case of a disease which usually terminates fatally, it is evident that the probability of survival of the individual in question is diminished, it is singularly difficult to use that kind of proof in the case of affliction not of the kind to bring on death directly. There is, indeed, only one objective way of proving that individuals have fewer chances of survival in certain conditions than in others, and that is simply to show that, actually, most of them do nòt live as long. Now, if in the case of purely individual pathology this demonstration is often possible, it is entirely impracticable in social pathology. For here the data at the disposal of the biologist, namely, the average rate of mortality, is wanting. We cannot determine approximately the moments of the birth and death of a society. All these problems, which are far from being solved in biology, are still more mysterious to the sociologist. Moreover, the events occurring in the course of social life and repeating themselves almost identically in all societies of the same type are much too varied for anyone to be able to determine in what measure one of them has contributed to hasten the end. Since individuals are very numerous, we can exercise a selection and compare only those who have a single irregularity in common; this factor is then isolated from all concomitant factors. It is thereby possible to study its influence on the organism. If, for example, a thousand rheumatic patients, chosen at random, present a mortality appreciably higher than the average, there is good reason for attributing this result to that disease. But in sociology, as each social species contains but a small number of individual groups, the field of possible comparisons is too restricted to make demonstrations of this kind valid.

Now, in the absence of such empirical proof, only deductive reasonings are possible, whose conclusions can have no other than presumptive value. We then prove not that a given event actually does weaken the social organism, but that it "must" logically have that effect. In order to prove this, we affirm that it entails a certain consequence judged as harmful to society; and for this reason it is called morbid. But even granted that it actually produces this consequence, it is possible that this disturbance is compensated, and even overcompensated, for by advantages that are overlooked. Further, there is only one possible reason for characterizing the aforementioned consequence as harmful, namely, that it disturbs the normal functioning of society. Such a proof, however, presupposes that the problem has already been solved; for such could be the case only if one has determined in advance what is normal, together with the distinctive criteria by which normality can be identified. It is unnecessary to discuss here the value of a wholly aprioristic construction of the concept of normality. Thus in sociology, as in history, the same events may be characterized, according to the personal sentiments of the scholar, either as beneficial or disastrous. Irreligious writers describe as abnormal the remnants of faith surviving in the midst of the general upheaval of religious beliefs; while to the religious individual, unbelief (agnosticism) is the great social malady of today. Similarly, to the socialist the present economic organization is a monstrosity, while to the orthodox economist it is the socialist tendencies that are pathological par excellence. And to support its opinions each party finds reasonings which it considers well argued.

The common flaw in these definitions is their premature attempt to grasp the essence of phenomena. They presuppose propositions which, true or not, can be proved only at a more advanced stage of science. This is just the case where we should apply the rule previously established. Instead of aspiring to determine at the outset the relations of the normal and the morbid to vital forces, let us simply seek some external and perceptible characteristic which will enable us merely to distinguish these two orders of facts.

All sociological phenomena (as well as all biological phenomena) can assume different forms in different cases while still conserving their essential characteristics. We can distinguish two kinds of such forms. Some are distributed in the entire range of the species; they are to be found, if not in all individuals, at least in the majority of them. If they are not found to be identical in all the cases in question, but vary in different persons, these variations do occur within narrow limits. There are, of course, exceptional variations besides these; but these are, first, to be found only in the minority of cases; and, secondly, where they do occur, they most often do not persist throughout the life of the individual. They are an exception both in time and in space.[1] Here are, then, two distinct varieties of phenomena to which we ought to assign different terms. We shall call "normal" these social conditions that are the most generally distributed, and the others "morbid" or "pathological." If we

[1] Hereby one can distinguish the morbid case from the monstrosity. The second is an exception in space only; it is not met with in the average of the species, but it persists throughout the life of the individual in which it is found. These two orders of facts differ, however, only in degree, and are fundamentally of the same nature; their boundaries are very uncertain, for morbidity is capable of permanence and monstrosity of modification. They can, then, scarcely be rigidly separated in their definitions. The distinction between them cannot be more categorical than that between the morphological and the physiological, since, in short, the morbid is the abnormal in the physiological order as the monstrous is the abnormal in the anatomical order.

designate as "average type" that hypothetical being that is constructed by assembling in the same individual, the most frequent forms, one may say that the normal type merges with the average type, and that every deviation from this standard of health is a morbid phenomenon. It is true that the average type cannot be determined with the same distinctness as an individual type, since its constituent attributes are not absolutely fixed but are likely to vary. But the possibility of its constitution is beyond doubt, since, blending as it does with the generic type, it is the immediate subject matter of science. It is the functions of the average organism that the physiologist studies; and the sociologist does the same. Once we know how to distinguish the various social species one from the other—a problem which will be treated below—it is always possible to find the most general form of a phenomenon in a given species.

It is clear that a condition can be defined as pathological only in relation to a given species. The conditions of health and morbidity cannot be defined in the abstract and absolutely. This rule is not denied in biology; it has never occurred to anyone to assume that what is normal for a mollusk is normal also for a vertebrate. Each species has a health of its own, because it has an average type of its own. Hence, there exists a state of health for the lowest species as well as for the highest. The same principle applies to sociology, although it is often misunderstood here. One should completely abandon the still too widespread habit of judging an institution, a practice or a moral standard as if it were good or bad in and by itself, for all social types indiscriminately.

Since the point of reference for judging health or morbidity varies with the species, it varies also for a single species, if this species itself changes. Thus, from the purely biological point of view, what is normal for the savage is not always normal for the civilized man, and vice versa.[2] There are, especially, the variations depending on age, which are important because they occur regularly in all species. The health of the aged person is not that of the adult, and, similarly, the health of the latter is not that of the child; the same is true of societies.[3] A social fact can, then, be called normal for a given social species only in relation to a given phase of its development; consequently, to know if it has a right to this appellation, it is not enough to observe the form it takes in the generality of societies belonging to this species; we must also take special care to consider them at the corresponding phase of their evolution.

It may seem that we have simply given a definition of terms, for we have only grouped phenomena according to their resemblances and differences, and given names to the groups thus formed. But, in reality, the concepts thus constituted, while having the great advantage of being recognizable by objective and readily perceptible characteristics, do not differ from the lay conception of health and morbidity. Is not morbidity commonly regarded as an accident which the living organism endures but does not itself ordinarily produce? That is what the ancient philosophers meant when they said that it does not originate from the nature of things—that it is the result of some circumstance

[2] For example, a savage with the undersized digestive system and the overdeveloped nervous system of the healthy civilized man would be ill in relation to his environment.

[3] We cut short this part of our discussion since we can only repeat here, with regard to social facts in general, what we have said elsewhere on the subject of the division of moral facts into normal and abnormal ones. (See *Division du travail social*, pp. 33–39.)

in the organism. Such a conception is, surely, a negation of all science; for morbidity is no more miraculous than is health: it is equally grounded in the nature of things. But it is not grounded in their normal nature; it is not inherent in their ordinary constitution or bound up with the conditions of existence upon which they generally depend. Conversely, nobody distinguishes the type of the healthy specimen from the type of the species. One cannot, without contradiction, even conceive of a species which would be incurably diseased in itself and by virtue of its fundamental constitution. The healthy constitutes the norm par excellence and can consequently be in no way abnormal.

Health is also commonly thought of as a state generally preferable to morbidity. But this definition is already implied in the preceding one. There must, indeed, have been some reason by virtue of which the characteristics, which in the aggregate form the normal type, have been able to spread to the entire species. This dissemination is itself a fact in need of explanation, and a cause must therefore be assigned to it. It would be incomprehensible if the most widespread forms of organization would not at the same time be, *at least in their aggregate*, the most advantageous. How could they have maintained themselves under so great a variety of circumstances if they had not enabled the individual better to resist the elements of destruction? On the other hand, the reason for the rarity of the other characteristics is evidently that the average organism possessing them has greater difficulty in surviving. The greater frequency of the former is, thus, a proof of their superiority.[4]

[4] M. Garofalo has tried to distinguish between the morbid and the abnormal (*Criminologie*, pp. 109, 110). But he bases this distinction exclusively on the following two arguments: (1) The word "morbidity" always signifies

II

This last statement furnishes a means of checking the results of the preceding method.

Since the general distribution of normal phenomena is itself an explainable phenomenon, after it has been definitely established by observation it should be explained. Although it is assumed, of course, that it is not without its cause, science demands that we know exactly what this cause is. The normality of the phenomenon will, indeed, be more certain if it is demonstrated that the external sign, which had at first revealed it, is not purely adventitious but grounded in the nature of things—if, in a word, one can erect this normality of fact into a normality by logical necessity. Furthermore, this demonstration will not always consist in showing that the trait is useful to the organism, although this is most frequently the case; but it can also happen, as we have remarked above, that a situation is normal without being at all useful, simply because it is necessarily implied in the nature of the being. Thus, it would perhaps be desirable if parturition did not occasion such violent disturbances in the female organism, but this is impossible;

---

something tending toward the total or partial destruction of the organism; if there is not destruction, there is cure, but never stability, as in some anomalies. But we have just seen that the abnormal is a menace to the living being, on the average. It is true that this is not always the case, but the dangers of morbidity likewise exist only in average cases. And if the absence of stability is taken as the criterion of the morbid, chronic morbidities are overlooked, and the monstrosity is completely separated from the pathological. Monstrosities are fixed. (2) We are told that the normal and the abnormal vary with races, whereas the distinction between the physiological and the pathological holds good for the entire human race. But we have just shown, on the contrary, that often phenomena which are morbid for the savage are not morbid for the civilized man. The conditions of physical health vary with the group.

consequently, the normality of the phenomenon is to be explained by the mere fact that it is bound up with the conditions of existence of the species under consideration, either as a mechanically necessary effect of these conditions or as a means permitting the organisms to adapt themselves.[5]

This proof is not simply useful as a check. It must not be forgotten that, if there is any advantage in distinguishing the normal from the abnormal, it is especially helpful in making our practice more intelligent. To act with full knowledge of the facts, we need to know not only the proper procedure but also the reasons for it. Scientific propositions concerning the normal state will be more immediately applicable to individual cases when accompanied by their reasons, for then we shall be better able to recognize in which cases, and in which direction, they should be modified in their application.

There are circumstances in which this verification is absolutely necessary, since the first method, if used alone, might lead to error. This applies to periods of transition, when the entire species is in process of evolution, without having yet become stabilized in its new form. The only normal type that is valid under such circumstances is the type from the previous condition, and yet it no longer corresponds to the new conditions of existence.

A phenomenon can thus persist throughout the entire range of a species although no longer adapted to the requirements of the situation. It is then normal only in appearance. Its universality is now an illusion, since its persistence, due

5 One may well ask whether the necessary derivation of a phenomenon from the general conditions of life does not imply its utility. We cannot treat at length this philosophical question, which will, however, be touched on below.

only to the blind force of habit, can no longer be accepted as an index of a close connection with the general conditions of its collective existence. This difficulty is especially peculiar to sociology. It scarcely exists in biology. Very rarely, indeed, are animal species compelled to take on unforeseen forms. The only normal modifications they undergo are those occurring regularly in each individual, principally under the influence of age. Therefore, the norm is easily established, since it can be observed in a great many cases. The normal state can be known at each moment of the development of the animal and even in periods of crisis, and the same is also true in sociology for societies belonging to the lower cultures. Since many of them have already completed their cycle of development, the law of their normal evolution is (or, at least, can be) established. For the highest and most recent societies this law is by definition unknown, since they have not yet accomplished their entire course. Having no point of reference, the sociologist may then be embarrassed in deciding whether a phenomenon is normal or not.

The procedure just indicated will free him from this difficulty. After having established by observation that a particular fact is general, he will go back to the conditions which determined this generality in the past and will then investigate whether these conditions are still given in the present or if, on the contrary, they have changed. In the first case he may properly designate the phenomenon as normal; and, in the second, refuse it this designation. For example, in order to determine whether the present economic state of Europe, with the absence of organization[6] characterizing it, is normal or not, we shall investigate the causes

[6] Cf., on this point, the note we published in the *Revue philosophique*, November, 1893, on "La Définition du socialisme."

which brought it about. If these conditions still exist in our present-day society, this situation is normal in spite of the dissent it arouses. But if, on the contrary, it is found to be related to the old social structure which we have elsewhere qualified as segmental[7] and which, after having been the essential framework of societies, progressively disappears, we shall have to conclude that the present situation, however universal, is pathological. By the same method should be settled all controversial questions of this kind, such as those concerning the normality of the decline in religious beliefs or of the development of state powers.[8]

[7] Segmental societies and, more particularly, segmental societies with a territorial basis are those whose essential boundaries correspond to territorial divisions. (See *Division du travail social*, pp. 189–210.)

[8] In certain cases, one can proceed in a slighly different way and prove, in the case of a fact whose normality is doubted, the validity or invalidity of this suspicion by showing its close connection with the previous development of the social type under consideration, and even to social evolution in general. Or one can show the opposite, that it contradicts both. In this way we have been able to prove that the present weakening of religious beliefs, and more generally of collective sentiments, is only normal; we have proved that this weakening becomes more and more accentuated as societies approach our present type and as the latter, in its turn, is more highly developed (*ibid.*, pp. 73–182). But, fundamentally, this method is only a particular case of the preceding one. For this demonstration of the normality of the phenomenon in question implies that we relate it to the most general conditions of our collective existence. Indeed, on the one hand, the positive correlation between this regression of religious consciousness and the degree of articulation of the structure of our societies is based not on some accidental cause but on the very constitution of our social milieu. Since, on the other hand, the traits characteristic of this constitution are certainly more highly developed today than formerly, it is only normal that the phenomena depending on it be themselves more highly developed. This method differs from the preceding one only in one feature, namely, that the conditions explaining and justifying the generality of the phenomenon are inferred and not directly observed. We know that it is connected with the nature of the social milieu without knowing the nature and mode of this connection.

Nevertheless, this method can by no means be substituted for the preceding one, nor even be employed as a first resort. In the first place, it raises questions which we shall treat below and which can be approached only at a rather advanced stage of science, for it implies, on the whole, an almost complete explanation of the phenomena concerned, and assumes that either their causes or their functions have already been determined. Now, it is important, from the very beginning of research, to be able to classify facts as normal and abnormal, save for a few exceptional cases, so that the proper domains can be assigned to physiology and pathology, respectively. Further, it is in relation to the normal type that a fact must be useful or necessary, if it is to be designated as normal itself. Otherwise it could be demonstrated that morbidity is indistinguishable from health, since it is merely an outgrowth of the afflicted organism. In this case, however, it is morbid because it does not maintain its proper relation to the average organism. Similarly, since a remedy is useful to the sick, its application could then be considered as a normal phenomenon. The remedy itself possesses this utility. One can, then, use this further method only after the normal type has been determined by some previous method. Finally and above all, if it is true that all that is normal is useful, without being necessary, it is not true that all that is useful is normal. Certainly the states that have become general in the species are more useful than those that have remained exceptional, but they do not possess the maximum of utility that exists or might possibly be brought about. We have no reason to believe that all possible combinations have been tried out in the course of experience; and, among those conceivable but never realized, there are some that are perhaps much more advantageous than those now known to us. The idea of utility is broader than that of normality; it has to the latter the same relation as the genus to the species. It is impossible to deduce the greater from the less, the genus from the species. But the species, since it is contained in the genus, can be discovered in the latter. That is why, once the generality of the phenomenon has been established, one can, by showing its utility, confirm the results of the first method.[9] We may, therefore, formulate the three following rules:

1. *A social fact is normal, in relation to a given social type at a given phase of its development, when it is present in the average society of that species at the corresponding phase of its evolution.*

2. *One can verify the results of the preceding method by showing that the generality of the phenomenon is bound up with the general conditions of collective life of the social type considered.*

3. *This verification is necessary when the fact in question occurs in a social species which has not yet reached the full course of its evolution.*

III

The custom of resolving these difficult questions with a pat phrase and of deciding hastily, from superficial observa-

[9] But it will be said that the determination of the normal type is not the highest objective possible and that, in order to transcend it, science has to be transcended also. We are avowedly not concerned with this question here; let us answer only: (1) that the question is entirely theoretical, for the normal type, the state of health, is difficult enough to determine and rarely enough attained for us to search our imagination in the attempt to find something better; (2) that these improvements of the normal type, although objectively advantageous, are not objectively desirable for that reason, for, if they do not correspond to a latent or actual tendency, they add nothing to happiness, and, if they do, the normal type is not realized; (3) and finally, that in order to improve the normal type, it must be known. One can, then, in any case, only transcend science by first making the best possible use of it.

tions supported by syllogisms, whether a social fact is normal or not prevails to such an extent that our procedure will perhaps be judged needlessly complicated. It seems unnecessary to go to such lengths in order to distinguish between morbidity and health. It is true that we make these distinctions every day, but it remains to be seen whether we make them correctly. The fact that the biologist solves these problems with relative ease obscures in our minds the difficulties they involve. We forget that it is much easier for him than for the sociologist to observe how the resistance of the organism is affected by each phenomenon and to determine thereby its normal or abnormal character with sufficient exactness for practical purposes. In sociology the greater complexity and inconstancy of the facts oblige us to take many more precautions, and this is all too evident in the contradictory judgments on the same phenomenon given by different scholars. In order to show clearly the great necessity for circumspection, we shall illustrate by a few examples the errors resulting from the opposite attitude and show in how different a light the most essential phenomena appear when treated methodically.

If there is any fact whose pathological character appears incontestable, that fact is crime. All criminologists are agreed on this point. Although they explain this pathology differently, they are unanimous in recognizing it. But let us see if this problem does not demand a more extended consideration.

We shall apply the foregoing rules. Crime is present not only in the majority of societies of one particular species but in all societies of all types. There is no society that is not confronted with the problem of criminality. Its form changes; the acts thus characterized are not the same everywhere; but, everywhere and always, there have been men who have behaved in such a way as to draw upon themselves penal repression. If, in proportion as societies pass from the lower to the higher types, the rate of criminality, i.e., the relation between the yearly number of crimes and the population, tended to decline, it might be believed that crime, while still normal, is tending to lose this character of normality. But we have no reason to believe that such a regression is substantiated. Many facts would seem rather to indicate a movement in the opposite direction. From the beginning of the [nineteenth] century, statistics enable us to follow the course of criminality. It has everywhere increased. In France the increase is nearly 300 per cent. There is, then, no phenomenon that presents more indisputably all the symptoms of normality, since it appears closely connected with the conditions of all collective life. To make of crime a form of social morbidity would be to admit that morbidity is not something accidental, but, on the contrary, that in certain cases it grows out of the fundamental constitution of the living organism; it would result in wiping out all distinction between the physiological and the pathological. No doubt it is possible that crime itself will have abnormal forms, as, for example, when its rate is unusually high. This excess is, indeed, undoubtedly morbid in nature. What is normal, simply, is the existence of criminality, provided that it attains and does not exceed, for each social type, a certain level, which it is perhaps not impossible to fix in conformity with the preceding rules.[10]

[10] From the fact that crime is a phenomenon of normal sociology, it does not follow that the criminal is an individual normally constituted from the biological and psychological points of view. The two questions are independent of each other. This independence will be better understood when we have shown, later on, the difference between psychological and sociological facts.

Here we are, then, in the presence of a conclusion in appearance quite paradoxical. Let us make no mistake. To classify crime among the phenomena of normal sociology is not to say merely that it is an inevitable, although regrettable phenomenon, due to the incorrigible wickedness of men; it is to affirm that it is a factor in public health, an integral part of all healthy societies. This result is, at first glance, surprising enough to have puzzled even ourselves for a long time. Once this first surprise has been overcome, however, it is not difficult to find reasons explaining this normality and at the same time confirming it.

In the first place crime is normal because a society exempt from it is utterly impossible. Crime, we have shown elsewhere, consists of an act that offends certain very strong collective sentiments. In a society in which criminal acts are no longer committed, the sentiments they offend would have to be found without exception in all individual consciousnesses, and they must be found to exist with the same degree as sentiments contrary to them. Assuming that this condition could actually be realized, crime would not thereby disappear; it would only change its form, for the very cause which would thus dry up the sources of criminality would immediately open up new ones.

Indeed, for the collective sentiments which are protected by the penal law of a people at a specified moment of its history to take possession of the public conscience or for them to acquire a stronger hold where they have an insufficient grip, they must acquire an intensity greater than that which they had hitherto had. The community as a whole must experience them more vividly, for it can acquire from no other source the greater force necessary to control these individuals who formerly were the most refractory. For

murderers to disappear, the horror of bloodshed must become greater in those social strata from which murderers
are recruited; but, first it must become greater throughout
the entire society. Moreover, the very absence of crime
would directly contribute to produce this horror; because
any sentiment seems much more respectable when it is
always and uniformly respected.

One easily overlooks the consideration that these strong
states of the common consciousness cannot be thus reinforced without reinforcing at the same time the more feeble
states, whose violation previously gave birth to mere infrac-
tion of convention—since the weaker ones are only the
prolongation, the attenuated form, of the stronger. Thus
robbery and simple bad taste injure the same single al-
truistic sentiment, the respect for that which is another's.
However, this same sentiment is less grievously offended by
bad taste than by robbery; and since, in addition, the average consciousness has not sufficient intensity to react keenly
to the bad taste, it is treated with greater tolerance. That
is why the person guilty of bad taste is merely blamed,
whereas the thief is punished. But, if this sentiment grows
stronger, to the point of silencing in all consciousnesses
the inclination which disposes man to steal, he will become
more sensitive to the offenses which, until then, touched
him but lightly. He will react against them, then, with
more energy; they will be the object of greater opprobrium,
which will transform certain of them from the simple
moral faults that they were and give them the quality of
crimes. For example, improper contracts, or contracts
improperly executed, which only incur public blame or
civil damages, will become offenses in law.

Imagine a society of saints, a perfect cloister of exemplary
individuals. Crimes, properly so called, will there be un-

known; but faults which appear venial to the layman will create there the same scandal that the ordinary offense does in ordinary consciousnesses. If, then, this society has the power to judge and punish, it will define these acts as criminal and will treat them as such. For the same reason, the perfect and upright man judges his smallest failings with a severity that the majority reserve for acts more truly in the nature of an offense. Formerly, acts of violence against persons were more frequent than they are today, because respect for individual dignity was less strong. As this has increased, these crimes have become more rare; and also, many acts violating this sentiment have been introduced into the penal law which were not included there in primitive times.[11]

In order to exhaust all the hypotheses logically possible, it will perhaps be asked why this unanimity does not extend to all collective sentiments without exception. Why should not even the most feeble sentiment gather enough energy to prevent all dissent? The moral consciousness of the society would be present in its entirety in all the individuals, with a vitality sufficient to prevent all acts offending it—the purely conventional faults as well as the crimes. But a uniformity so universal and absolute is utterly impossible; for the immediate physical milieu in which each one of us is placed, the hereditary antecedents, and the social influences vary from one individual to the next, and consequently diversify consciousnesses. It is impossible for all to be alike, if only because each one has his own organism and that these organisms occupy different areas in space. That is why, even among the lower peoples, where individual originality is very little developed, it nevertheless does exist.

[11] Calumny, insults, slander, fraud, etc.

Thus, since there cannot be a society in which the individuals do not differ more or less from the collective type, it is also inevitable that, among these divergences, there are some with a criminal character. What confers this character upon them is not the intrinsic quality of a given act but that definition which the collective conscience lends them. If the collective conscience is stronger, if it has enough authority practically to suppress these divergences, it will also be more sensitive, more exacting; and, reacting against the slightest deviations with the energy it otherwise displays only against more considerable infractions, it will attribute to them the same gravity as formerly to crimes. In other words, it will designate them as criminal.

Crime is, then, necessary; it is bound up with the fundamental conditions of all social life, and by that very fact it is useful, because these conditions of which it is a part are themselves indispensable to the normal evolution of morality and law.

Indeed, it is no longer possible today to dispute the fact that law and morality vary from one social type to the next, nor that they change within the same type if the conditions of life are modified. But, in order that these transformations may be possible, the collective sentiments at the basis of morality must not be hostile to change, and consequently must have but moderate energy. If they were too strong, they would no longer be plastic. Every pattern is an obstacle to new patterns, to the extent that the first pattern is inflexible. The better a structure is articulated, the more it offers a healthy resistance to all modification; and this is equally true of functional, as of anatomical, organization. If there were no crimes, this condition could not have been fulfilled; for such a hypothesis presupposes that collective sentiments have arrived at a degree of intensity unexampled in history. Nothing is good indefinitely and to an unlimited extent. The authority which the moral conscience enjoys must not be excessive; otherwise no one would dare criticize it, and it would too easily congeal into an immutable form. To make progress, individual originality must be able to express itself. In order that the originality of the idealist whose dreams transcend his century may find expression, it is necessary that the originality of the criminal, who is below the level of his time, shall also be possible. One does not occur without the other.

Nor is this all. Aside from this indirect utility, it happens that crime itself plays a useful role in this evolution. Crime implies not only that the way remains open to necessary changes but that in certain cases it directly prepares these changes. Where crime exists, collective sentiments are sufficiently flexible to take on a new form, and crime sometimes helps to determine the form they will take. How many times, indeed, it is only an anticipation of future morality —a step toward what will be! According to Athenian law, Socrates was a criminal, and his condemnation was no more than just. However, his crime, namely, the independence of his thought, rendered a service not only to humanity but to his country. It served to prepare a new morality and faith which the Athenians needed, since the traditions by which they had lived until then were no longer in harmony with the current conditions of life. Nor is the case of Socrates unique; it is reproduced periodically in history. It would never have been possible to establish the freedom of thought we now enjoy if the regulations prohibiting it had not been violated before being solemnly abrogated. At that time, however, the violation was a crime, since it was an offense against sentiments still very keen in the average conscience. And yet this crime was useful as a prelude to reforms which daily became more necessary. Liberal philosophy had as its precursors the heretics of all kinds who were justly punished by secular authorities during the entire course of the Middle Ages and until the eve of modern times.

From this point of view the fundamental facts of criminality present themselves to us in an entirely new light. Contrary to current ideas, the criminal no longer seems a totally unsociable being, a sort of parasitic element, a strange and unassimilable body, introduced into the midst of society.[12] On the contrary, he plays a definite role in social life. Crime, for its part, must no longer be conceived as an evil that cannot be too much suppressed. There is no occasion for self-congratulation when the crime rate drops noticeably below the average level, for we may be certain that this apparent progress is associated with some social disorder. Thus, the number of assault cases never falls so low as in times of want.[13] With the drop in the crime rate, and as a reaction to it, comes a revision, or the need of a revision in the theory of punishment. If, indeed, crime is a disease, its punishment is its remedy and cannot be other-

[12] We have ourselves committed the error of speaking thus of the criminal, because of a failure to apply our rule (*Division du travail social*, pp. 395–96).

[13] Although crime is a fact of normal sociology, it does not follow that we must not abhor it. Pain itself has nothing desirable about it; the individual dislikes it as society does crime, and yet it is a function of normal physiology. Not only is it necessarily derived from the very constitution of every living organism, but it plays a useful role in life, for which reason it cannot be replaced. It would, then, be a singular distortion of our thought to present it as an apology for crime. We would not even think of protesting against such an interpretation, did we not know to what strange accusations and misunderstandings one exposes oneself when one undertakes to study moral facts objectively and to speak of them in a different language from that of the layman.

wise conceived; thus, all the discussions it arouses bear on the point of determining what the punishment must be in order to fulfil this role of remedy. If crime is not pathological at all, the object of punishment cannot be to cure it, and its true function must be sought elsewhere.

It is far from the truth, then, that the rules previously stated have no other justification than to satisfy an urge for logical formalism of little practical value, since, on the contrary, according as they are or are not applied, the most essential social facts are entirely changed in character. If the foregoing example is particularly convincing—and this was our hope in dwelling upon it—there are likewise many others which might have been cited with equal profit. There is no society where the rule does not exist that the punishment must be proportional to the offense; yet, for the Italian school, this principle is but an invention of jurists, without adequate basis.[14]

For these criminologists the entire penal system, as it has functioned until the present day among all known peoples, is a phenomenon contrary to nature. We have already seen that, for M Garofalo, the criminality peculiar to lower societies is not at all natural. For socialists it is the capitalist system, in spite of its wide diffusion, which constitutes a deviation from the normal state, produced, as it was, by violence and fraud. Spencer, on the contrary, maintains that our administrative centralization and the extension of governmental powers are the radical vices of our societies, although both proceed most regularly and generally as we advance in history. We do not believe that scholars have ever systematically endeavored to distinguish the normal or abnormal character of social phenomena from their degree

[14] See Garofalo, *Criminologie*, p. 299.

of generality. It is always with a great array of dialectics that these questions are partly resolved.

Once we have eliminated this criterion, however, we are not only exposed to confusions and partial errors, such as those just pointed out, but science is rendered all but impossible. Its immediate object is the study of the normal type. If, however, the most widely diffused facts can be pathological, it is possible that the normal types never existed in actuality; and if that is the case, why study the facts? Such study can only confirm our prejudices and fix us in our errors. If punishment and the responsibility for crime are only the products of ignorance and barbarism, why strive to know them in order to derive the normal forms from them? By such arguments the mind is diverted from a reality in which we have lost interest, and falls back on itself in order to seek within itself the materials necessary to reconstruct its world. In order that sociology may treat facts as things, the sociologist must feel the necessity of studying them exclusively.

The principal object of all sciences of life, whether individual or social, is to define and explain the normal state and to distinguish it from its opposite. If, however, normality is not given in the things themselves—if it is, on the contrary, a character we may or may not impute to them—this solid footing is lost. The mind is then complacent in the face of a reality which has little to teach it; it is no longer restrained by the matter which it is analyzing, since it is the mind, in some manner or other, that determines the matter.

The various principles we have established up to the present are, then, closely interconnected. In order that sociology may be a true science of things, the generality of phenomena must be taken as the criterion of their normality.

Our method has, moreover, the advantage of regulating action at the same time as thought. If the social values are not subjects of observation but can and must be determined by a sort of mental calculus, no limit, so to speak, can be set for the free inventions of the imagination in search of the best. For how may we assign to perfection a limit? It escapes all limitation, by definition. The goal of humanity recedes into infinity, discouraging some by its very remoteness and arousing others who, in order to draw a little nearer to it, quicken the pace and plunge into revolutions. This practical dilemma may be escaped if the desirable is defined in the same way as is health and normality and if health is something that is defined as inherent in things. For then the object of our efforts is both given and defined at the same time. It is no longer a matter of pursuing desperately an objective that retreats as one advances, but of working with steady perseverance to maintain the normal state, of re-establishing it if it is threatened, and of rediscovering its conditions if they have changed. The duty of the statesman is no longer to push society toward an ideal that seems attractive to him, but his role is that of the physician: he prevents the outbreak of illnesses by good hygiene, and he seeks to cure them when they have appeared.[15]

[15] From the theory developed in this chapter, the conclusion has at times been reached that, according to us, the increase of criminality in the course of the nineteenth century was a normal phenomenon. Nothing is farther from our thought. Several facts indicated by us apropos of suicide (see *Suicide*, pp. 420 ff.) tend, on the contrary, to make us believe that this development is in general morbid. Nevertheless, it might happen that a certain increase of certain forms of criminality would be normal, for each state of civilization has its own criminality. But on this, one can only formulate hypotheses.

CHAPTER IV

RULES FOR THE CLASSIFICATION
OF SOCIAL TYPES

Since a social fact can be construed as normal or abnormal only relatively to a given social species, it is implied that one branch of sociology must be devoted to the constitution and classification of these species.

This concept of the social species has the very great advantage of furnishing us a middle ground between the two opposite conceptions of collective life which have for a long time divided the ranks of scholars: the nominalism of historians,[1] and the extreme realism of philosophers. For the historian, societies represent just so many heterogeneous individualities, not comparable among themselves. Each people has its own physiognomy, its special constitution, its law, its morality, its economic organization, appropriate only to itself; and all generalizations are well-nigh impossible. For the philosopher, on the contrary, all these individual groupings, called tribes, city-states, and nations, are only contingent and provisional aggregations with no exclusive and separate reality. Only humanity is real, and it is from the general attributes of human nature that all social evolution flows.

For the former, consequently, history is but a sequence of events which follow without repeating one another; for the latter, these same events have value and interest only

[1] I call it thus because it has been frequent among historians, but I do not mean that it is found in all historians.

as illustrating the general laws inherent in the constitution of man and dominating all historical development. For the former, what is good for one society cannot be applied to others. The conditions of the state of health vary from one people to the next and cannot be theoretically determined; it is a matter of practical experience and of cautious research. For the latter, they can be calculated once and for all and for the entire human species. It seems, then, that social reality must be merely subject matter of an abstract and vague philosophy or for purely descriptive monographs. But one escapes from this alternative once one has recognized that, between the confused multitude of historic societies and the single, but ideal, concept of humanity, there are intermediaries, namely, social species. In the latter are united both the unity that all truly scientific research demands and the diversity that is given in the facts, since the species is the same for all the individual units that make it up, and since, on the other hand, the species differ among themselves. It remains true that moral, legal, and economic institutions, etc., are infinitely variable; but these variations are not of such a nature that they deny all scientific treatment.

It was because he failed to appreciate the existence of social species that Comte thought he could represent the progress of all human societies as identical with that of a single people "to which would be ideally transferred all the consecutive modifications observed in distinct peoples."[2] If one single social species exists, individual societies can differ among themselves only in degree, according as they present more or less completely the component traits of this unique species, i. e., according as they express humanity

[2] *Cours de philosophie positive*, IV, 263.

more or less perfectly. If, on the contrary, social types exist, qualitatively distinct from one another, one will try in vain to draw them together. They cannot be joined like the identical sections of a straight line in geometry. Historical development thus loses the ideal and simple continuity attributed to it; it breaks up, so to speak, into a multitude of fragments which, because they specifically differ from one another, cannot be joined together in a unified manner. The famous metaphor of Pascal, which has since been repeated by Comte, is, from this point of view, entirely untrue.

But how shall we constitute these species?

I

It may seem, at the outset, that no other manner of procedure exists than to study each particular society, to make as exact and complete a monograph of it as possible, then to compare all these monographs among themselves to see wherein they are the same and wherein they diverge, and then, according to the relative importance of these similarities and divergences, to classify the peoples into groups according to their similarities or differences. In support of this method, we may say that it is the only method acceptable in a science of observation. If the species is only the sum of individual societies, how, then, can we describe it if one does not begin by describing each one of them and by describing them completely? Is it not the rule in science to rise to the general only after having observed the particular and that in its entirety? For this reason it has sometimes been thought necessary to postpone sociological analysis to the infinitely distant date when history, in its study of particular societies, will have arrived at results sufficiently objective and definite to be capable of useful comparison.

But, in reality, this circumspection is scientific in appearance only. It is not true that science can institute laws only after having reviewed all the facts they express, and can establish classes only after having described, in their entirety, the individuals they comprise. The true experimental method tends rather to substitute for common sense facts (which provide proofs only when they are very numerous and which, consequently, permit conclusions that are always doubtful)—*decisive* or crucial facts, which, by themselves and independently of their number, have scientific value and interest, as Bacon has pointed out.[3] This procedure is especially important when it is a question of constituting genera and species. For, to make an inventory of all the characteristics belonging to an individual is an impossible task. Every individual is an infinity, and infinity cannot be exhausted. Shall they confine themselves to the most essential properties? But by what principle shall the choice be made? For such purposes a criterion which extends beyond the individual is necessary; such a criterion even the best-constructed monographs could not supply. Without even carrying matters to this extreme, we can foresee that, as the characteristics which form the basis of the classification become more numerous, it will also be more difficult to find resemblances and differences sufficiently distinct to permit the constitution of definite groups and subgroups because of the diverse ways in which they combine in individual cases.

But even if a classification by this method were possible, it would have the very great failing of not rendering the services which are expected from it. A satisfactory method must, above all, aim at facilitating scientific work by sub-

[3] *Novum organum*, Vol. II, § 36.

stituting a limited number of types for the indefinite multiplicity of individuals. But it loses this advantage if the types have only been constituted after all the individuals have been reviewed and entirely analyzed. It can scarcely facilitate research if it only sums up researches already accomplished. It will only be truly useful if it permits us to classify other characteristics than those serving as its basis and if it procures for us a framework for the facts to come. Its role is to put in our hands points of reference to which we can refer other observations than those which have furnished us with these very points of reference. But for this purpose it must be made not from a complete inventory of all the individual characteristics but from a small number of them, carefully chosen. Under these conditions it will serve not only to put into some order knowledge already acquired but also to make new knowledge. It will spare the observer many steps because it will guide him wisely. Once the classification is established on this principle, in order to know whether a fact is general throughout a species it will be unnecessary to observe all societies of this species; a few will suffice. Even one well-made observation will be enough in many cases, just as one well-constructed experiment often suffices for the establishment of a law.

We must, then, choose the most essential characteristics for our classification. It is true that we can know them only when the explanation of the facts is sufficiently advanced. These two parts of the science are inseparable, and each progresses through the other. Without entering, however, too far into the study of the facts, it is not difficult to conjecture in what quarter we must seek the characteristic properties of the social types. We know that societies are composed of various parts in combination. Since the nature of the aggregate depends necessarily on *the nature and number of the component elements and their mode of combination*, these characteristics are evidently what we must take as our basis; and we shall see from what follows that it is on them that the general facts of social life depend. Moreover, as they are of the morphological order, one could call the part of sociology which has for its task the constitution and classification of social types, "social morphology."

The principle of this classification can be given even greater precision. We know, indeed, that the constituent parts of every society are societies more simple than itself. A people is produced by the union of two or more pre-existent peoples. If, then, we understand the most simple society that has ever existed, to make our classification we should have only to follow the way these simple societies form compounds and how these compound societies combine again to form more complex wholes.

II

Spencer understood very well that the methodical classification of social types could have no other foundation. "We have seen," he said, "that social evolution begins with small, simple aggregates; that it progresses by the clustering of these into larger aggregates; and that after being consolidated, such clusters are united with others like themselves into still larger aggregates. Our classification, then, must begin with the societies of the first or simplest order."[4]

Unfortunately, to put this principle into practice it would be necessary to begin by defining with precision what is meant by a simple society. Not only does Spencer omit this definition, but he believes that it is almost impossible to make

[4] *Sociology*, I, 550.

it.[5] The fact is that simplicity, as he understands it, consists essentially in a certain crudity of organization. It is not easy to say with exactitude at what moment social organization is rudimentary enough to be called simple; this is a matter of evaluation. Also, the formula for it is so indeterminate that it fits all sorts of societies. "Our only course is to regard as a simple society, one which forms a single working whole unsubjected to any other, and of which the parts co-operate with or without a regulating centre, for certain public ends."[6] Unfortunately, many peoples satisfy this condition. Thus he includes, somewhat at random, under this same rubric all societies that are civilized only to a small extent. Given this point of departure, the possibilities of all the rest of his classification can easily be imagined. In truly astonishing confusion most dissimilar societies are brought together: the Homeric Greeks are placed parallel with the holders of feudal estates in the tenth century, and below the Bechuanas, the Zulus, and the Fijians; the Athenian confederation is parallel to the feudal estates of thirteenth-century France, and below the Iroquois and the Araucanians.

The definite meaning of the term "simplicity" can be no other than that of a complete absence of parts. A simple society is, then, a society which does not include others more simple than itself, and which not only at present contains but a single segment but also presents no trace of previous segmentation. The *"horde,"* as we have elsewhere defined it,[7] corresponds exactly to this definition. It is a social aggregate which does not include, and has never included,

[5] "We cannot in all cases say with precision what constitutes a simple society" (*ibid.*).

[6] *Ibid.*, p. 551.

[7] *Division du travail social*, p. 189.

within itself any other more elementary aggregate, but is directly composed of individuals. The latter do not form, within the total group, special groups differing from the whole; they are in atomic juxtaposition. Plainly a simpler society is impossible; the horde is thus the protoplasm of the social realm and, consequently, the natural basis of classification.

It is true, perhaps, that no historical society corresponds exactly to this description; but, as we have shown in the book cited above, we know many which are formed immediately and without intermediate groups by a combination of hordes. A horde which has thus become a social segment, instead of constituting an entire society, is called a clan; but it retains the same characteristic features. The clan is, indeed, a social aggregate which is not reducible to any other narrower one. It will, perhaps, be objected that the clan, where it is observed today, generally includes a number of families. But, first of all, we believe, for reasons we cannot develop here, that the formation of these small family groups is later than that of the clan; and further, they do not constitute social segments, in the proper sense of the term, because they are not political divisions. In all cases encountered, the clan constitutes the ultimate division of this genus. Consequently, even if no other facts substantiated the existence of the horde—and some such facts, which we shall one day have the opportunity to expound, are known to us—the existence of clans, that is, of societies formed by the compounding of hordes, authorizes us to suppose that there were at first simpler societies which may be reduced to the horde, properly so called. This would then make of the horde the seed from which all social species have developed.

Once this notion of the horde or single-segment society has been established—whether it be conceived as a historic reality or as a hypothesis of science—we have the support necessary for constructing the complete scale of social types. As many fundamental types will be distinguished as there are ways for the horde to combine and give birth to new societies and for the new societies to combine among themselves. We shall first meet aggregates formed simply by the combination of hordes or clans (to give them their new name) when they are in simple juxtaposition like the individuals of a horde. Examples of these, which one could term "simple polysegmental," are found in certain Iroquois and Australian tribes. The Kabyle tribe has the same character: it is a union of clans organized in the form of villages. Very probably, there was a moment in history when the Roman *curia* and the Athenian phratry were societies of this kind. Above these would be placed the societies formed by a union of societies of the preceding species, that is, "polysegmental societies simply compounded." Such is the character of the Iroquois confederation and of the confederation formed by the union of the Kabyle tribes. The same was true, at their origin, of each of the primitive tribes whose association later gave rise to the Roman city-state. We would then encounter the "polysegmental societies doubly compounded," which result from the juxtaposition or fusion of several simply compounded polysegmented societies. Such is the city-state, an aggregate of tribes, which are themselves aggregates of *curiae*, which, in their turn, resolve themselves into gentes, or clans; and the Germanic tribe, with its counties, which are subdivided into hundreds, which, in their turn, have as the final unit the clan, which has become a village.

We need not develop these few indications further, since

our task is not here to carry out a classification of societies. It is too complex a problem to be treated adequately in the space at our disposal; it presupposes an accumulation of long and special researches. We only wished, by a few examples, to make our ideas clear and to show how this principle of method must be applied. We should not even consider the foregoing as constituting a complete classification of the lower societies. We have somewhat simplified the matter for the sake of greater clarity. We have assumed, for example, that each higher type was formed by a combination of identical societies, namely, the type immediately below. Now it is quite possible that societies of different kinds, situated at unequal levels on the genealogical tree of social types, should unite in a way to form a new species. We know at least one case of this; that is, the Roman Empire, which embraced peoples most diverse in nature.[8]

But these types once constituted, there will be occasion for distinguishing different varieties in each one of them according as the segmental societies, which serve to form the resultant society, maintain a certain individuality or are, on the contrary, absorbed in the total mass. It is clear, indeed, that social phenomena vary not only with the nature of the component elements of society but also with their mode of composition; they will especially be very different according to whether each of the subgroups keeps its local life or is drawn into the general life—in other words, according to their degree of concentration. Consequently, we shall have to investigate whether, at any moment, a complete coalescence of these segments is produced. We can recognize such coalescence by the fact that the original constitution of the

[8] Nevertheless, it is probable that in general the distance between the component societies could not be very great; otherwise, there could be no cultural unity among them.

segment no longer affects its administrative and political organization. From this point of view the city-state is clearly distinct from the Germanic tribe. In the latter the organization, with clans as a basis, has maintained itself, although obscured toward the end of their history; while at Rome and Athens, the gentes and the γένη ceased very early to be political divisions and became private groups.

With the method thus outlined, it would be justifiable to introduce new distinctions on the basis of secondary morphological characteristics. However, for reasons that we shall give below, we believe it scarcely possible or useful to go beyond the general divisions just indicated. We need not enter into these details, however, but content ourselves with having formulated the principle of classification, which may be enunciated as follows: *We shall begin by classifying societies according to the degree of organization they present, taking as a basis the perfectly simple society or the society of one segment. Within these types we shall distinguish different varieties according to whether a complete coalescence of the initial segments does or does not appear.*

III

These rules answer implicitly a question the reader has perhaps put to himself as he has followed this discussion: How can we deal with social species as if there were such things without having directly established their existence? The answer is contained in the very method just described.

We have seen that societies are only different combinations of one and the same original society. Now the same element can combine only with others like it; and the compounds which result can, in their turn, combine only among themselves by following a limited number of combinations, especially when the compound elements are few, as is the case with social segments. The gamut of possible combinations is therefore finite, and consequently most of them will necessarily appear repeatedly. We must therefore conclude that social species exist. Although the possibility remains that certain of these combinations are produced only once, this does not prevent its being a species. We shall simply say in cases of this kind that the species includes only one individual.[9]

There are social species, then, for the same reason that there are biological species. The latter are due to the fact that all organisms are merely varied combinations within one and the same anatomical unit. Nevertheless, there is, from this point of view, a greater difference between these two realms. In animals there is an exclusive trait which lends to their characteristics a fixity and permanence which is not found in the social species, namely, the capacity to reproduce. Because they are common to all members of a given species, the characteristics of animals are firmly rooted in the organism and are not readily modified by the action of the respective environments but persist uniformly in spite of the diversity of external circumstances. There is an internal force, heredity, that keeps them constant in spite of the external stimuli which oppose it. That is why they are clearly evident and can be determined with precision. In the social realm this internal force is lacking. As a rule, a second generation is a different species from the parent-societies because the latter, in combining, give birth to an entirely new organization. Only colonization can be compared to reproduction by germination; and in order that the type may persist, the colonial society must not mix with any other society of a different species or variety. The distinctive

[9] Is this not the case with the Roman Empire, which indeed appears to be without a parallel in history?

traits of the species do not then receive by heredity a reserve vitality which permits them to resist the pressure toward individual variation. They are modified in infinitely small gradations under the action of circumstances. Further, when we wish to discover the types by eliminating all variants, we often obtain only infinite forms. This indeterminateness increases naturally with the complexity of its characteristics. The more complex a thing is, the more numerous are the possible combinations from its parts. As a result the specific type does not present contours as definite as in biology except for the simplest and most general characteristics.[10]

[10] When we edited this chapter for the first edition of this work, we said nothing of the method of classifying species according to their state of civilization. At that time classifications of that type, proposed by authoritative sociologists, did not exist, save perhaps the too evidently archaic one of Comte. Since that time, several attempts have been made in this direction, more particularly the one by Vierkandt ("Die Kulturtypen der Menschheit," in *Archiv. f. Anthropologie*, 1898), by Sutherland (*The Origin and Growth of the Moral Instinct*), and by Steinmetz ("Classification des types sociaux," in *Année sociologique*, III, 43–147). Nevertheless, we shall not pause to discuss them, for they do not answer the problem stated in this chapter. One finds classified there, not social species, but historical phases, which is quite different. Since its origin, France has passed through very different forms of civilization; it began by being agricultural, passed to craft industry and to small commerce, then to manufacturing, and finally to large-scale industry. Now, it is impossible to admit that the same collective individuality can change its species three or four times. A species must define itself by more constant characteristics. The economic state, technological state, etc., present phenomena too unstable and complex to furnish the basis of a classification. It is even very probable that the same industrial, scientific, and artistic civilization can be found in societies whose hereditary constitution is very different. Japan may in the future borrow our arts, our industry, even our political organization; it will not cease to belong to a different social species from France and Germany. Let us add that these attempts, although conducted by sociologists of worth, have given only vague, indecisive results of little utility.

CHAPTER V

RULES FOR THE EXPLANATION
OF SOCIAL FACTS

The establishment of species is, above all, a means of grouping facts in order to facilitate their interpretation. But social morphology is only an introduction to the truly explanatory part of the science. What is the proper method of this part?

I

Most sociologists think they have accounted for phenomena once they have shown how they are useful, what role they play, reasoning as if facts existed only from the point of view of this role and with no other determining cause than the sentiment, clear or confused, of the services they are called to render. That is why they think they have said all that is necessary, to render them intelligible, when they have established the reality of these services and have shown what social needs they satisfy.

Thus Comte traces the entire progressive force of the human species to this fundamental tendency "which directly impels man constantly to ameliorate his condition, whatever it may be, under all circumstances";[1] and Spencer relates this force to the need for greater happiness. It is in accordance with this principle that Spencer explains the formation of society by the alleged advantages which result from co-operation; the institution of government, by the utility of the regularization of military co-operation;[2] the transforma-

[1] *Cours de philosophie positive*, IV, 262.
[2] *Principles of Sociology*, II, 247.

tions through which the family has passed, by the need for reconciling more and more perfectly the interests of parents, children, and society.

But this method confuses two very different questions. To show how a fact is useful is not to explain how it originated or why it is what it is. The uses which it serves presuppose the specific properties characterizing it but do not create them. The need we have of things cannot give them existence, nor can it confer their specific nature upon them. It is to causes of another sort that they owe their existence. The idea we have of their utility may indeed motivate us to put these forces to work and to elicit from them their characteristic effects, but it will not enable us to produce these effects out of nothing. This proposition is evident so long as it is a question only of material, or even psychological, phenomena. It would be equally evident in sociology if social facts, because of their extreme intangibility, did not wrongly appear to us as without all intrinsic reality. Since we usually see them as a product purely of mental effort, it seems to us that they may be produced at will whenever we find it necessary. But since each one of them is a force, superior to that of the individual, and since it has a separate existence, it is not true that merely by willing to do so may one call them into being. No force can be engendered except by an antecedent force. To revive the spirit of the family, where it has become weakened, it is not enough that everyone understand its advantages; the causes which alone can engender it must be made to act directly. To give a government the authority necessary for it, it is not enough to feel the need for this authority; we must have recourse to the only sources from which all authority is derived. We must, namely, establish traditions, a common spirit, etc.; and for this it is necessary again to go back along the chain of causes and effects until we find a point where the action of man may be effectively brought to bear.

What shows plainly the dualism of these two orders of research is that a fact can exist without being at all useful, either because it has never been adjusted to any vital end or because, after having been useful, it has lost all utility while continuing to exist by the inertia of habit alone. There are, indeed, more survivals in society than in biological organisms. There are even cases where a practice or a social institution changes its function without thereby changing its nature. The rule, *Is pater quem justae nuptiae declarant*,[3] has remained in our code essentially the same as it was in the old Roman law. While its purpose then was to safe-guard the property rights of a father over children born to the legitimate wife, it is rather the rights of children that it protects today. The custom of taking an oath began by being a sort of judiciary test and has become today simply a solemn and imposing formality. The religious dogmas of Christianity have not changed for centuries, but the role which they play is not the same in our modern societies as in the Middle Ages. Thus, the same words may serve to express new ideas. It is, moreover, a proposition true in sociology, as in biology, that the organ is independent of the function—in other words, while remaining the same, it can serve different ends. The causes of its existence are, then, independent of the ends it serves.

Nevertheless, we do not mean to say that the impulses, needs, and desires of men never intervene actively in social evolution. On the contrary, it is certain that they can hasten or retard its development, according to the circumstances

---

[3] Legal marriage with the mother establishes the father's rights over the children.

which determine the social phenomena. Apart from the fact that they cannot, in any case, make something out of nothing, their actual intervention, whatever may be its effects, can take place only by means of efficient causes. A deliberate intention can contribute, even in this limited way, to the production of a new phenomenon only if it has itself been newly formed or if it is itself a result of some transformation of a previous intention. For, unless we postulate a truly providential and pre-established harmony, we cannot admit that man has carried with him from the beginning—potentially ready to be awakened at the call of circumstances —all the intentions which conditions were destined to demand in the course of human evolution. It must further be recognized that a deliberate intention is itself something objectively real; it can, then, neither be created nor modified by the mere fact that we judge it useful. It is a force having a nature of its own; for that nature to be given existence or altered, it is not enough that we should find this advantageous. In order to bring about such changes, there must be a sufficient cause.

For example, we have explained the constant development of the division of labor by showing that it is necessary in order that man may maintain himself in the new conditions of existence as he advances in history. We have attributed to this tendency, which is rather improperly named the "instinct of self-preservation," an important role in our explanations. But, in the first place, this instinct alone could not account for even the most rudimentary specialization. It can do nothing if the conditions on which the division of labor depends do not already exist, i.e., if individual differences have not increased sufficiently as a consequence of the progressive disintegration of the common consciousness and of hereditary influences.[4] It was even necessary that division of labor should have already begun to exist for its usefulness to be seen and for the need of it to make itself felt. The very development of individual differences, necessarily accompanied by a greater diversity of tastes and aptitudes, produced this first result. Further, the instinct of self-preservation did not, of itself and without cause, come to fertilize this first germ of specialization. We were started in this new direction, first, because the course we previously followed was now barred and because the greater intensity of the struggle, owing to the more extensive consolidation of societies, made more and more difficult the survival of individuals who continued to devote themselves to unspecialized tasks. For such reasons it became necessary for us to change our mode of living. Moreover, if our activity has been turned toward a constantly more developed division of labor, it is because this was also the direction of least resistance. The other possible solutions were emigration, suicide, and crime. Now, in the average case, the ties attaching us to life and country and the sympathy we have for our fellows are sentiments stronger and more resistant than the habits which could deflect us from narrower specialization. These habits, then, had inevitably to yield to each impulse that arose. Thus the fact that we allow a place for human needs in sociological explanations does not mean that we even partially revert to teleology. These needs can influence social evolution only on condition that they themselves, and the changes they undergo, can be explained solely by causes that are deterministic and not at all purposive.

But what is even more convincing than the preceding con-

[4] *Division du travail*, Book II, chaps. iii and iv.

siderations is a study of actual social behavior. Where purpose reigns, there reigns also a more or less wide contingency; for there are no ends, and even fewer means, which necessarily control all men, even when it is assumed that they are placed in the same circumstances. Given the same environment, each individual adapts himself to it according to his own disposition and in his own way, which he prefers to all other ways. One person will seek to change it and make it conform to his needs; another will prefer to change himself and moderate his desires. To arrive at the same goal, many different ways can be and actually are followed. If, then, it were true that historic development took place in terms of ends clearly or obscurely felt, social facts should present the most infinite diversity; and all comparison should be almost impossible.

To be sure, the external events which constitute the superficial part of social life vary from one people to another, just as each individual has his own history, although the bases of physical and moral organization are the same for all. But when one comes in contact with social phenomena, one is, on the contrary, surprised by the astonishing regularity with which they occur under the same circumstances. Even the most minute and the most trivial practices recur with the most astonishing uniformity. A certain nuptial ceremony, purely symbolical in appearance, such as the carrying-off of the betrothed, is found to be exactly the same wherever a certain family type exists; and again this family type itself is linked to a whole social organization. The most bizarre customs, such as the couvade, the levirate, exogamy, etc., are observed among the most diverse peoples and are symptomatic of a certain social state. The right to make one's will appears at a certain phase of history, and the more or less important restrictions limiting it offer a fairly exact clue to the particular stage of social evolution. It would be easy to multiply examples. This wide diffusion of collective forms would be inexplicable if purpose or final causes had the predominant place in sociology that is attributed to them.

When, then, the explanation of a social phenomenon is undertaken, we must seek separately the efficient cause which produces it and the function it fulfils. We use the word "function," in preference to "end" or "purpose," precisely because social phenomena do not generally exist for the useful results they produce. We must determine whether there is a correspondence between the fact under consideration and the general needs of the social organism, and in what this correspondence consists, without occupying ourselves with whether it has been intentional or not. All these questions of intention are too subjective to allow of scientific treatment.

Not only must these two types of problems be separated, but it is proper, in general, to treat the former before the latter. This sequence, indeed, corresponds to that of experience. It is natural to seek the causes of a phenomenon before trying to determine its effects. This method is all the more logical since the first question, once answered, will often help to answer the second. Indeed, the bond which unites the cause to the effect is reciprocal to an extent which has not been sufficiently recognized. The effect can doubtless not exist without its cause; but the latter, in turn, needs its effect. It is from the cause that the effect draws its energy; but it also restores it to the cause on occasion, and consequently it cannot disappear without the cause showing the effects of its disappearance.[5]

For example, the social reaction that we call "punishment" is due to the intensity of the collective sentiments which the crime offends; but, from another angle, it has the useful function of maintaining these sentiments at the same degree of intensity, for they would soon diminish if offenses against them were not punished.[6] Similarly, in proportion as the social milieu becomes more complex and more unstable, traditions and conventional beliefs are shaken, become more indeterminate and more unsteady, and reflective powers are developed. Such rationality is indispensable to societies and individuals in adapting themselves to a more mobile and more complex environment.[7] And again, in proportion as men are obliged to furnish more highly specialized work, the products of this work are multiplied and are of better quality; but this increase in products and improvement in quality are necessary to compensate for the expense which this more considerable work entails.[8] Thus, instead of the cause of social phenomena consisting of a mental anticipation of the function they are called to fill, this function, on the contrary, at least in a number of cases, serves to maintain the pre-existent cause from which they are derived. We shall, then, find the function more easily if the cause is already known.

If the determination of function is thus to be delayed, it

[5] We do not wish to raise here questions of general philosophy, which would not be in place. Let us say, however, that, if more profoundly analyzed, this reciprocity of cause and effect might furnish a means of reconciling scientific mechanism with the teleology which the existence, and especially the persistence, of life implies.

[6] *Division du travail social*, Book II, chap. ii, notably pp. 105 ff.

[7] *Ibid.*, pp. 52–53.　　　　　　　　[8] *Ibid.*, pp. 301 ff.

is still no less necessary for the complete explanation of the phenomena. Indeed, if the usefulness of a fact is not the cause of its existence, it is generally necessary that it be useful in order that it may maintain itself. For the fact that it is not useful suffices to make it harmful, since in that case it costs effort without bringing in any returns. If, then, the majority of social phenomena had this parasitic character, the budget of the organism would have a deficit and social life would be impossible. Consequently, to have a satisfactory understanding of the latter, it is necessary to show how the phenomena comprising it combine in such a way as to put society in harmony with itself and with the environment external to it. No doubt, the current formula, which defines social life as a correspondence between the internal and the external milieu, is only an approximation; however, it is in general true. Consequently, to explain a social fact it is not enough to show the cause on which it depends; we must also, at least in most cases, show its function in the establishment of social order.

II

Having distinguished between these two approaches, we must determine the method by which they may be developed. At the same time that it is teleological, the method of explanation generally followed by sociologists is essentially psychological. These two tendencies are interconnected with one another. In fact, if society is only a system of means instituted by men to attain certain ends, these ends can only be individual, for only individuals could have existed before society. From the individual, then, have emanated the needs and desires determining the formation of societies; and, if it is from him that all comes, it is necessarily by him that all must be explained. Moreover, there are in societies only individual consciousnesses; in these, then, is found the source of all social evolution.

Hence, sociological laws can be only a corollary of the more general laws of psychology; the ultimate explanation of collective life will consist in showing how it emanates from human nature in general, whether the collective life be deduced from human nature directly and without previous observation or whether it must be related to human nature after the latter has been analyzed.

These terms are almost literally those used by Auguste Comte to characterize his method. "Since," says he, "the social phenomenon, conceived in its totality, is fundamentally *only a simple development of humanity, without the creation of any special faculties whatsoever*, as I have established above, all the effective dispositions that sociological investigation will successively discover will therefore be found at least in the germ in this primordial type which biology has constructed in advance for sociology."[9] According to him, the predominant fact in social life is progress; and moreover, progress depends on an exclusively psychological factor, namely, the tendency which impels man to perfect his nature more and more. Social facts would then be derived so directly from human nature that during the first phases of history they might be directly deduced from it without the necessity of having recourse to the observation of society.[10] It is true that, as Comte confesses, it is impossible to apply this deductive method to the more advanced periods of evolution. But this impossibility is purely a practical one. It is due to the fact that the distance between the point of departure and the point of arrival becomes so consider-

[9] *Op. cit.*, IV, 333.   [10] *Ibid.*, p. 345.

able that the human mind risks going astray, if it undertakes to traverse it without a guide.[11] But the relation between the fundamental laws of human nature and the ultimate products of social progress does not cease to be intimate. The most complex forms of civilization are only a development of the psychological life of the individual. Thus, while the theories of psychology are insufficient as premises for sociological reasoning, they are the touchstone which alone can test the validity of propositions inductively established. "A law of social succession," says Comte, "even when indicated with all possible authority by the historical method, ought to be finally admitted only after having been rationally related to the positive theory of human nature, either in a direct or indirect way."[12] Psychology, then, will always have the last word.

Such is likewise the method followed by Spencer. Indeed, according to him, the two primary factors of social phenomena are the external environment and the physical and social constitution of the individual.[13] Now, the former can influence society only through the latter, which thus becomes the essential force of social evolution. If society is formed, it is in order to permit the individual to express his nature; and all the transformations through which this nature has passed have no other object than to make this expression easier and more complete. It is by reason of this principle that, before proceeding to his research in social organization, Spencer thought it necessary to devote almost the entire first volume of his *Principles of Sociology* to the study of the physical, emotional, and intellectual aspects of primitive man. "The science of sociology," he says, "sets out

11 *Ibid.*, p. 346.   12 *Ibid.*, p. 335.
13 *Principles of Sociology*, Vol. I, Part I, chap. ii.

with social units, conditioned as we have seen, constituted physically, emotionally, and intellectually, and possessed of certain early acquired notions and correlative feelings."[14] And it is in two of these feelings—fear of the living and fear of the dead—that he finds the origin of political and religious government.[15] He admits, it is true, that once it is formed society reacts on individuals.[16] But it does not follow that society itself has the power of directly engendering the smallest social fact; from this point of view it exerts an effect only by the intermediation of the changes it effects in the individual. It is, then, always in human nature, whether original or acquired, that everything is based. Moreover, this action that the social body exercises on its members cannot be at all specific, since political ends have no separate existence but are simply a summary statement of human needs.[17] It can then be only a duplication of private activity. In industrial societies, particularly, we are unable to see where social influence has a place, since the object of these societies is, precisely, to liberate the individual and his natural impulses by ridding him of all social constraint.

This principle is not only at the basis of these great doctrines of general sociology, but it likewise fathers an equally large number of specific theories. Thus, domestic organization is commonly explained by the sentiment parents have for their children, and children for their parents; the institution of marriage, by the advantages it presents

[14] *Ibid.*, p. 437.   [15] *Ibid.*, p. 437.   [16] *Ibid.*, p. 14.

[17] "Society exists for the benefit of its members; not its members for the benefit of society . . . . the claims of the body politic are nothing in themselves, and become something only in so far as they embody the claims of its component individuals" (*ibid.*, Part II, pp. 461-62).

for the married pair and their progeny; punishment, by the anger which every grave attack upon his interests causes in the individual. All economic life, as economists of the orthodox school especially conceive and explain it, is definitely dependent upon a purely individual factor, the desire for wealth. In morality, the duty of the individual toward himself is made the basis of all ethics. As for religion, it becomes a product of the impressions which the great forces of nature or of certain eminent personalities awaken in man, etc.

But, if such a method is applied to social phenomena, it changes fundamentally their nature. To prove this, let us recall the definition we have given. Since their essential characteristic is their power of exerting pressure on individual consciousnesses, it follows that they are not derived from the latter and, consequently, that sociology is not a corollary of individual psychology. For this power of constraint is evidence of the fact that social phenomena possess a different nature from ours, since they control us only by force or, at the very least, by weighing upon us more or less heavily. If social life were merely an extension of the individual being, it would not thus ascend toward its source, namely, the individual, and impetuously invade it. If the authority before which the individual bows when he acts, feels, or thinks socially governs him to this extent, it does so because it is a product of social forces which transcend him and for which he, consequently, cannot account. The external impulse to which he submits cannot come from him, nor can it be explained by what happens within him. It is true that we are not incapable of self-control; we can restrain our impulses, habits, and even instincts, and can arrest their development by an act of inhibition. But these inhibitory movements should not be confused with those constituting social constraint. The process of the former is centrifugal; of the latter, centripetal. The former are elaborated in the individual consciousness and then tend to externalize themselves; the latter are at first external to the individual, whom they then tend to fashion in their image from without. Inhibition is, if you like, the means by which social constraint produces its psychological effects; it is not identical with this constraint.

When the individual has been eliminated, society alone remains. We must, then, seek the explanation of social life in the nature of society itself. It is quite evident that, since it infinitely surpasses the individual in time as well as in space, it is in a position to impose upon him ways of acting and thinking which it has consecrated with its prestige. This pressure, which is the distinctive property of social facts, is the pressure which the totality exerts on the individual.

But, it will be said that, since the only elements making up society are individuals, the first origins of sociological phenomena cannot but be psychological. In reasoning thus, it can be established just as easily that organic phenomena may be explained by inorganic phenomena. It is very certain that there are in the living cell only molecules of crude matter. But these molecules are in contact with one another, and this association is the cause of the new phenomena which characterize life, the very germ of which cannot possibly be found in any of the separate elements. A whole is not identical with the sum of its parts. It is something different, and its properties differ from those of its component parts. Association is not, as has sometimes been believed, merely an infertile phenomenon; it is not simply the putting of facts and constituent properties into juxtaposition. On the contrary, it is the source of all the innovations which have been produced successively in the course of the general evolution of things. What differences are there between the lower and higher organisms, between highly organized living things and protoplasm, between the latter and the inorganic molecules of which it is composed, if not differences in types of association? All these beings, in the last analysis, resolve themselves into the same elements, but these elements are here in mere juxtaposition, there in combination, here associated in one way, there in another. One may even inquire whether this law does not apply in the mineral world and whether the differences separating inorganic bodies are not traceable to this same origin.

By reason of this principle, society is not a mere sum of individuals. Rather, the system formed by their association represents a specific reality which has its own characteristics. Of course, nothing collective can be produced if individual consciousnesses are not assumed; but this necessary condition is by itself insufficient. These consciousnesses must be combined in a certain way; social life results from this combination and is, consequently, explained by it. Individual minds, forming groups by mingling and fusing, give birth to a being, psychological if you will, but constituting a psychic individuality of a new sort.[18] It is, then,

[18] In this sense, and for these reasons, one can, and must, speak of a collective consciousness distinct from individual consciousnesses. In order to justify this distinction, it is not necessary to posit for the former a separate personal existence; it is something special and must be designated by a special term, simply because the states which constitute it differ specifically from those which constitute the individual consciousnesses. This specificity comes from the fact that they are not formed from the same elements. The latter result from the nature of the organicopsychological being taken in isolation,

in the nature of this collective individuality, not in that of the associated units, that we must seek the immediate and determining causes of the facts appearing therein. The group thinks, feels, and acts quite differently from the way in which its members would were they isolated. If, then, we begin with the individual, we shall be able to understand nothing of what takes place in the group. In a word, there is between psychology and sociology the same break in continuity as between biology and the physicochemical sciences. Consequently, every time that a social phenomenon is directly explained by a psychological phenomenon, we may be sure that the explanation is false.

Our critics will perhaps maintain that although society, once formed, is the proximate cause of social phenomena, the causes determining its formation may still be psychological in nature. They grant that, when individuals are associated, their association can give rise to a new form of life; but they claim that the new form can take place only for reasons inherent in individuals. But, in reality, as far back as one goes in history, the principle of association is the most imperative of all, for it is the source of all other compulsions. As a consequence of my birth, I am obliged to associate with a given group. It may be said that later, as an adult, I acquiesce in this obligation by the very fact that I continue to live in my country. But what difference does that make? This "acquiescence" is still imperative. Pressure accepted and submitted to with good grace is still pressure. Moreover, let us look more closely at the nature of my acquies-

---

the former from the combination of a plurality of beings of this kind. The resultants cannot, then, fail to differ, since the components differ to that extent. Our definition of the social fact, moreover, only drew in another way this line of demarcation.

cence. For the present, it is most certainly imposed upon me, for in the vast majority of cases it is materially and morally impossible for us to strip off our nationality; such a change is generally considered apostasy. Likewise in the past, which determines the present, I could not have given my free consent. I did not desire the education I received, which, more than any other thing, fixes me to my native soil. Finally, for the future, I cannot give my acquiescence, for I cannot know what the future is to be. I do not know all the duties which may be incumbent upon me at some future time in my capacity as a citizen. How could I acquiesce in them in advance?

We have shown, then, that the source of all that is obligatory is outside the individual. So long, then, as we do not desert the facts, the principle of association presents the same character as the others and, consequently, is explained in the same manner.

Moreover, as all societies are born of other societies without a break in continuity, we can be certain that in the entire course of social evolution there has not been a single time when individuals determined by careful deliberation whether or not they would enter into the collective life or into one collective life rather than another. In order for that question to arise, it would be necessary to go back to the first origins of all societies. But the questionable solutions which can be brought to such problems could not, in any case, affect the method by which we must treat the facts given in history. Therefore, we do not need to discuss them.

But one would be strangely mistaken about our thought if, from the foregoing, he drew the conclusion that sociology, according to us, must, or even can, make an abstraction of man and his faculties. It is clear, on the contrary, that the general characteristics of human nature participate in the work of elaboration from which social life results. But they are not the cause of it, nor do they give it its special form; they only make it possible. Collective representations, emotions, and tendencies are caused not by certain states of the consciousnesses of individuals but by the conditions in which the social group in its totality is placed. Such actions can, of course, materialize only if the individual natures are not resistant to them; but these individual natures are merely the indeterminate material that the social factor molds and transforms. Their contribution consists exclusively in very general attitudes, in vague and consequently plastic predispositions which, by themselves, if other agents did not intervene, could not take on the definite and complex forms which characterize social phenomena.

What an abyss, for example, between the sentiments man experiences in the face of forces superior to his own and the present religious institution with its beliefs, its numerous and complicated practices, its material and moral organization! What a contrast between the psychic states of sympathy which two beings of the same blood experience for one another,[19] and the detailed collection of legal and moral regulations that determine the structure of the family, the relations of persons among themselves, of things with persons, etc.! We have seen that, even where society is reduced to an unorganized crowd, the collective sentiments which are formed in it may not only not resemble, but even be opposed to, the sentiments of the average individual. How much greater must be the difference between them when the pressure exerted on the individual is that of a well-organized

[19] We may suppose that this exists in lower social groups. See, on this point, Espinas, *Sociétés animales*, p. 474.

society, in which the action of the traditions of former generations is added to that of contemporaries! A purely psychological explanation of social facts cannot fail, therefore, to allow all that is characteristic (i.e., social) in them to escape.

What has blinded most sociologists to the inadequacy of this method is that, taking effect for cause, they have very often designated as determining the conditions of social phenomena certain psychological states that are relatively definite and distinctive but which are, after all, only the consequence of these social phenomena. Thus a certain religious sentiment has been considered innate in man, a certain minimum of sexual jealousy, filial piety, paternal love, etc. And it is by these that religion, marriage, and the family have been explained.

History, however, shows that these inclinations, far from being inherent in human nature, are often totally lacking. Or they may present such variations in different societies that the residue obtained after eliminating all these differences—which alone can be considered of psychological origin—is reduced to something vague and rudimentary and far removed from the facts that need explanation. These sentiments, then, *result* from the collective organization and are not its *basis*. It has not been proved at all that the tendency to gregariousness has been an inherited instinct of the human species from its beginnings. It is much more natural to consider it a product of social life, which was slowly developed within us; for it is a fact of observation that animals are or are not gregarious according to whether their habits oblige them to live a common life or to avoid it. We must add that the difference between even the more definite tendencies and social reality remains considerable.

There is, moreover, a way to isolate the psychological factor almost completely in such a manner as to determine precisely the extent of its action, viz., to see how race affects social evolution. Indeed, ethnic characteristics are organico-psychological in type. Social life must, therefore, vary when they vary, if psychological phenomena have on society the effects attributed to them. But no social phenomenon is known which can be placed in indisputable dependence on race. No doubt, we cannot attribute to this proposition the value of a principle; we can merely affirm it as invariably true in practical experience.

The most diverse forms of organization are found in societies of the same race, while striking similarities are observed between societies of different races. The city-state existed among the Phoenicians, as among the Romans and the Greeks; we find it in the process of formation among the Kabyles. The patriarchal family was almost as highly developed among the Jews as among the Hindus; but it is not found among the Slavs, who are, however, of the Aryan race. On the other hand, the family type met among Slavs also exists among the Arabs. The maternal family and the clan are observed everywhere. The detail of legal procedure and of nuptial ceremonies is the same among peoples most dissimilar from the ethnic point of view.

If all these things are true, it is because the psychological factor is too general to predetermine the course of social phenomena. Since it does not call for one social form rather than another, it cannot explain any of them. There are, it is true, a certain number of facts which are customarily attributed to the influence of race. In this manner is explained, notably, the rapid and intensive development of arts and letters in Athens, so slow and mediocre in Rome.

But this interpretation of the facts, although classical, has never been scientifically demonstrated; it seems, indeed, to derive all its authority solely from tradition. The possibility of a sociological explanation of the same phenomena has not been explored, but we are convinced that it could be attempted with success. In short, when the artistic character of Athenian civilization is related with such facility to inherited aesthetic faculties, we show as little insight as did scholars in the Middle Ages when they explained fire by phlogiston and the effects of opium by its dormitive property.

Finally, if social evolution really had its origin in the psychological constitution of man, its origin seems to be completely obscure. For we would then have to admit that its motivating force is some inner spring of human nature. But what could this be? Is it the sort of instinct Comte speaks of, which impels man more and more to express his nature? But that is begging the question and explaining progress by an innate "tendency toward progress"—a metaphysical entity of the very existence of which there is no demonstration. Even the highest animal species are not at all activated by the need to progress, and among human societies there are many which are content to remain indefinitely stationary.

Or is this motivating force, as Spencer seems to believe, the urge for greater happiness which the increasingly complex forms of civilization are designed to satisfy more and more completely? We would then have to establish the fact that happiness increases with civilization, and we have elsewhere described all the difficulties to which this hypothesis gives rise.[20] But further, even if one or the other of these

[20] *Division du travail social*, Book II, chap. i.

two postulates were admissible, historical development would not thereby be rendered intelligible, for the explanation which would result from it would be purely teleological. We have shown above that social facts, like all natural phenomena, are not explained by the simple consideration that they serve some end. When it has been proved satisfactorily that the progressively more intelligent social organizations which have succeeded one another in the course of history have had the effect of satisfying more and more certain of our fundamental desires, we have not shown at all how these social organizations have been produced. The fact that they were useful does not tell us how they originated. Even if we were to explain how we came to imagine them and how we planned them in advance so as to picture to ourselves their services to us—a somewhat difficult problem in itself—the desires which called forth their existence do not have the power of drawing them out of nothing. In a word, admitting that social organizations are the necessary means to attain a desired goal, the whole question remains: From what source and by what means have these been created?

We arrive, therefore, at the following principle: *The determining cause of a social fact should be sought among the social facts preceding it and not among the states of the individual consciousness.* Moreover, we see quite readily that all the foregoing applies to the determination of the function as well as the cause of social phenomena. The function of a social fact cannot but be social, i.e., it consists of the production of socially useful effects. To be sure, it may and does happen that it also serves the individual. But this happy result is not its immediate cause. We can then complete the preceding proposition by saying: *The function of a social fact ought always to be sought in its relation to some social end.*

Since sociologists have often misinterpreted this rule and have considered social phenomena from a too psychological point of view, to many their theories seem too vague and shifting and too far removed from the distinctive nature of the things they are intended to explain. Historians who treat social reality directly and in detail have not failed to remark how powerless these too general interpretations are to show the relation between the facts; and their mistrust of sociology has been, no doubt, partly produced by this circumstance. We do not mean to say, of course, that the study of psychological facts is not indispensable to the sociologist. If collective life is not derived from individual life, the two are nevertheless closely related; if the latter cannot explain the former, it can at least facilitate its explanation. First, as we have shown, it is indisputable that social facts are produced by action on psychological factors. In addition, this very action is similar to that which takes place in each individual consciousness and by which are transformed the primary elements (sensations, reflexes, instincts) of which it is originally constituted. Not without reason has it been said that the self is itself a society, by the same right as the organism, although in another way; and long ago psychologists showed the great importance of the factor of association in the explanation of mental activity.

Psychological training, more than biological training, constitutes, then, a valuable lesson for the sociologist; but it will not be useful to him except on condition that he emancipates himself from it after having received profit from its lessons, and then goes beyond it by special sociological training. He must abandon psychology as the center of his operations, as the point of departure for his excursions into the sociological world to which they must always return. He must establish himself in the very heart of social facts, in order to observe them directly, while asking the science of the individual mind for a general preparation only and, when needed, for useful suggestions[21]

III

Since the facts of social morphology are of the same nature as physiological phenomena, they must be explained by the principle just enunciated. All the preceding argument points to the fact that they play a preponderant role in collective life, and hence in sociological explanations.

In fact, if the determining condition of social phenomena is, as we have shown, the very fact of association, the phenomena ought to vary with the forms of that association, i.e., according to the ways in which the constituent parts of society are grouped. Since, moreover, a given aggregate, formed by the union of elements of all kinds which enter into the composition of a society, constitutes its internal en-

[21] Psychological phenomena can have only social consequences when they are so intimately united to social phenomena that the action of the psychological and of the social phenomena is necessarily fused. This is the case with certain sociopsychological facts. Thus, a public official is a social force, but he is at the same time an individual. As a result he can turn his social energy in a direction determined by his individual nature, and thereby he can have an influence on the constitution of society. Such is the case with statesmen and, more generally, with men of genius. The latter, even when they do not fill a social function, draw from the collective sentiments of which they are the object an authority which is also a social force, and which they can put, in a certain measure, at the service of personal ideas. But we see that these cases are due to individual accidents and, consequently, cannot affect the constitutive traits of the social species which, alone, is the object of science. The restriction on the principle enunciated above is not, then, of great importance for the sociologist.

vironment (just as the aggregate of anatomic elements, together with the way in which they are disposed in space, constitutes the internal milieu of organisms), we can say: *The first origins of all social processes of any importance should be sought in the internal constitution of the social group.*

It is possible to be even more precise. The elements which make up this milieu are of two kinds: things and persons. Besides material objects incorporated into the society, there must also be included the products of previous social activity: law, established customs, literary and artistic works, etc. But it is clear that the impulsion which determines social transformations can come from neither the material nor the immaterial, for neither possesses a motivating power. There is, assuredly, occasion to take them into consideration in the explanations one attempts. They bear with a certain weight on social evolution, whose speed and even direction vary according to the nature of these elements; but they contain nothing of what is required to put it in motion. They are the matter upon which the social forces of society act, but by themselves they release no social energy. As an active factor, then, the human milieu itself remains.

The principal task of the sociologist ought to be, therefore, to discover the different aspects of this milieu which can exert some influence on the course of social phenomena. Until the present, we have found two series of facts which have eminently fulfilled this condition; these are: (1) the number of social units or, as we have also called it, the "size of a society"; and (2) the degree of concentration of the group, or what we have termed the "dynamic density." By this last expression must not be understood the purely physical concentration of the aggregate, which can have no effect if the individuals, or rather the groups of individuals, remain separated by social distance. By it is understood the social concentration, of which the size is only the auxiliary and, generally speaking, the consequence. The dynamic density may be defined, the volume being equal, as the function of the number of individuals who are actually having not only commercial but also social relations, i.e., who not only exchange services or compete with one another but also live a common life. For, as purely economic relations leave men estranged from one another, there may be continuous relations of that sort without participation in the same collective existence. Business carried on across the frontiers which separate peoples does not abolish these frontiers.

Social life can be affected only by the number of those who participate effectively in it. That is why the dynamic density of a people is best expressed by the degree of fusion of the social segments. For, if each partial aggregate forms a whole, i.e., a distinct individuality separated by barriers from the others, the action of the members, in general, remains localized within it. If, on the contrary, these partial societies are, or tend to be, all intermingled within the total society, to that extent is the radius of social life extended.

As for physical density—if is understood thereby not only the number of inhabitants per unit area but the development of lines of communication and transmission—it progresses, *ordinarily*, at the same rate as the dynamic density and, *in general*, can serve to measure it. If the different parts of the population tend to draw closer together, it is inevitable that they will build roads which permit it. From another angle, relations can be established between distant points in the social mass only if distance is not an obstacle, i.e., if it is bridged. However, there are exceptions,[22] and we would lay ourselves open to a serious error if we always judged the social concentration of a society by the degree of its physical concentration. Roads, railroads, etc., can serve for commerce better than for the fusion of populations, of which they are only a very imperfect index. Such is the case in England, whose physical density is greater than that of France, but where the coalescence of social areas is much less advanced, as is proved by the persistence of local spirit and regional life.

We have shown elsewhere how all growth in the volume and dynamic density of societies modifies profoundly the fundamental conditions of collective existence by rendering social life more intense, by extending the horizon of thought and action of each individual. We need not return to the application we then made of this principle. Let us add only that it has helped us to treat not only the still very general question that was the object of this study but many other more special problems, and that we have thus been able to verify its correctness by a considerable number of experiments. Nevertheless, we are far from claiming that we have found all the peculiarities of the social medium which may contribute to the explanation of social facts. All that we can say is that these are the only ones we have observed and that we have not been led to seek others.

But the significance attributed by us to the social and, more particularly, the human milieu does not imply that

---

[22] We made the mistake, in our *Division du travail*, of presenting material density too much as the exact expression of dynamic density. Nevertheless, the substitution of the former for the latter is absolutely legitimate for whatever concerns the economic effects of the latter, e.g., the division of labor as a purely economic fact.

we must see in it a sort of ultimate and absolute fact beyond which there is no reason for inquiry. It is evident, on the contrary, that its condition at each moment of history is itself a result of social causes, some of which are inherent in the society itself, while others depend on interaction between this society and its neighbors. Moreover, science is not concerned with first-causes, in the absolute sense of the word. For science, a fact is primary simply when it is general enough to explain a great number of other facts. Now, the social milieu is certainly a factor of this kind, since the changes which are produced in it, whatever may be their causes, have their repercussions in all directions in the social organism and cannot fail to affect to some extent each of its functions.

What has just been said of the general social milieu can be repeated for the special milieus of each of the partial groups it comprises. For example, according as the family is large or small or lives a life more or less complete, domestic life will vary. Similarly, if professional groups extend their function over an entire territory instead of remaining restricted, as formerly, to the limits of a city, their professional activity will be very different from what it was formerly. More generally, professional life will be quite different according to whether the milieu of each profession is strongly restricted or whether it is unrestrained, as it is today. Nevertheless, the action of these particular milieus could not have the importance of the general milieu, for they are themselves subject to the influence of the latter. We must always return to the general milieus. The pressure it exerts on these partial groups modifies their organization.

This conception of the social milieu, as the determining factor of collective evolution, is of the highest importance.

For, if we reject it, sociology cannot establish any relations of causality. In fact, if we eliminate this type of cause, there are no concomitant conditions on which social phenomena can depend; for if the external social milieu, i.e., that which is formed by the surrounding societies, can take some action, it is only that of attack and defense; and, further, it can make its influence felt only by the intermediary of the internal social milieu. The principal causes of historical development would not be found, then, among the concomitant circumstances; they would all be in the past. They would themselves form a part of this development, of which they would constitute simply older phases. The present events of social life would originate not in the present state of society but in prior events, from historical precedents; and sociological explanations would consist exclusively in connecting the present with the past.

It may seem, it is true, that this is sufficient. Indeed, it is currently said that history has for its object precisely the linking of events in their order of succession. But it is impossible to conceive how the stage which a civilization has reached at a given moment could be the determining cause of the subsequent stage. The stages that humanity successively traverses do not engender one another. We understand that the progress achieved at a given epoch in the legal, economic, political field, etc., makes new progress possible; but how does it predetermine it? It is a point of departure which permits of further progress; but what incites us to such progress?

Are we to admit an inherent tendency which impels humanity ceaselessly to exceed its achievements either in order to realize itself completely or to increase its happiness; and is the object of sociology to rediscover the manner in which this tendency developed? Without returning to the difficulties such a hypothesis implies, in any case laws which would express this development cannot be at all causal, for relation of causality can be established only between two given facts. Now, this tendency, which is supposed to be the cause of this development, is not given; it is only postulated and constructed by the mind from the effects attributed to it. It is a sort of motivating faculty that we imagine as underlying movement, in order to account for it; but the efficient cause of a movement can only be another movement, not a potentiality of this kind.

All that we can observe experimentally in the species is a series of changes among which a causal bond does not exist. The antecedent state does not produce the subsequent one, but the relation between them is exclusively chronological. Under these circumstances, all scientific prevision is impossible. We can, indeed, say that certain conditions have succeeded one another up to the present, but not in what order they will henceforth succeed one another, since the cause on which they are supposed to depend is not scientifically determined or determinable. Ordinarily, it is true, we admit that evolution will take the same direction as in the past; but this is a mere postulate. Nothing assures us that the overt phenomena express so completely the nature of this tendency that we may be able to foretell the objective to which this tendency aspires as distinct from those through which it has successively passed. Why, indeed, should the direction it follows be rectilinear?

This is the reason for the restricted number of causal relations or laws established by sociology. With a few exceptions, of whom Montesquieu is the most illustrious example, the older philosophers of history tried solely to discover the general direction in which humanity orients itself, without seeking to relate the phases of this evolution to any concomitant condition. However great the services Comte has rendered to social philosophy, the terms in which he has stated the sociological problem do not differ from the preceding philosophers. Thus his famous law of the three stages of history has no relation of causality; if it is true, it is, and can be, only empirical. It is a bird's-eye view of the elapsed history of the human species. It is entirely arbitrary to consider the third stage as the definitive state of humanity. Who knows whether another will not emerge from it in the future?

Likewise the law which predominates in Spencer's sociology does not seem to be any different in its nature. If it were true that we tend at present to seek our happiness in an industrial civilization, nothing assures us that, in epochs to follow, we shall not seek it elsewhere. The prevalence and persistence of this method may be accounted for by the fact that we have usually seen in the social milieu a means by which progress is realized, not the cause which determines it.

From another angle, it is again with relation to this same milieu that the utility or, as we have called it, the function of social phenomena must be measured. Among the changes caused by the social milieu, only those serve a purpose which are compatible with the current state of society, since the milieu is the essential condition of collective existence. From this point of view again, the conception we have just expounded is, we believe, fundamental; for it alone enables us to explain how the useful character of social phenomena can vary, without however depending on a volitional social order. If we represent historic evolution as impelled by a sort of vital urge which pushes men forward, since a propelling tendency can have but one goal, there can be only one point of reference with relation to which the usefulness or harmfulness of social phenomena is calculated. Consequently, there can, and does, exist only one type of social organization that fits humanity perfectly; and the different historical societies are only successive approximations to this single model. It is unnecessary to show that, today, such a simple view is irreconcilable with the recognized variety and complexity of social forms. If, on the contrary, the fitness or unfitness of institutions can only be established in connection with a given milieu, since these milieus are diverse, there is a diversity of points of reference and hence of types which, while being qualitatively distinct from one another, are all equally grounded in the nature of the social milieus.

The question just treated is, then, closely connected with that of the constitution of social types. If there are social species, it is because collective life depends, above all, on concomitant conditions which present a certain diversity. If, on the contrary, all the principal causes of social events were in the past, each society would no longer be anything but the prolongation of its predecessor, and the different societies would lose their individuality and would become only diverse moments of one and the same evolution. Since, on the other hand, the constitution of the social milieu results from the mode of composition of the social aggregates—and these two expressions are essentially synonymous—we now have the proof that there are no more essential characteristics than those assigned by us as the basis of sociological classifications. Finally, we must now understand, better than previously, how unjust it would be for our critics to point to these words, "external conditions" and "milieu," as an accusation that our method seeks the sources of life outside the living being. On the contrary, the considerations just stated lead us back to the idea that the causes of social phenomena are internal to society. Rather, we ourselves could more justly criticize the theory which derives society from the individual for trying to extract the internal from the external (since it explains the social being by something other than itself) and the greater from the smaller (since it undertakes to deduce the whole from the part). So little have our principles misinterpreted the spontaneous character of every living being that, if we apply them to biology and psychology, we shall have to admit that there also the individual life is entirely developed within the individual.

IV

A certain conception of society and collective life emerges from the group of rules just established. But first let us set forth the contrary theories which divide opinion on this point. For some, such as Hobbes and Rousseau, there is a break in continuity between the individual and society. Man is thus naturally refractory to the common life; he can only resign himself to it when forced. Social ends are not simply the meeting-point of individual ends; they are, rather, contrary to them. Thus, to induce the individual to pursue them, it is necessary to constrain him; and the social task consists par excellence in the institution and organization of this constraint. Since, however, the individual is regarded as the sole reality of the human realm, this organization, having for its object to hinder and confine him, can only be conceived as artificial. It is not founded in nature, since this organization is destined to do human nature violence by preventing it from behaving in an antisocial manner. It is a work of art, a machine constructed entirely by hand of man, which, like all products of this kind, is only what it is because men have willed it so. A decree of the will created it; another can transform it.

Neither Hobbes nor Rousseau seems to have realized how contradictory it is to admit that the individual is himself the author of a machine which has for its essential role his domination and constraint. At least, it seemed to them sufficient for the elimination of this contradiction that it be disguised in the eyes of those who are its victims, by the clever artifice of the social contract.

It is from a quite different idea that the philosophers of natural law, the economists, and, more recently, Spencer[23] have taken their inspiration. For them social life is essentially spontaneous and society is a natural phenomenon. But, if they confer this character upon it, it is not because they find in it a specific nature but merely because they find its basis in the nature of the individual. No more than the aforementioned thinkers do they see in it a system of things existing separately, by reason of causes peculiar to itself. But, whereas the former conceived of it only as a conventional arrangement which is attached by no bond to reality and is supported in mid-air, so to speak, Spencer and the economists give as its bases the fundamental instincts of human nature. Man is naturally inclined to the political, domestic, and religious life, to commerce, etc.; and it is from these natural drives that social organization is derived. Consequently, wherever it is normal, it has no need to impose itself. When it has recourse to constraint, it is because it is not what it ought to be or because the circumstances are abnormal. In principle, we have only to leave individual

[23] The position of Comte on this matter is a rather ambiguous eclecticism.

forces to develop freely and they will tend to organize themselves socially. Neither one of these doctrines is ours. To be sure, we do make constraint the characteristic of all social facts. But this constraint does not result from more or less learned machinations, destined to conceal from men the traps in which they have caught themselves. It is due simply to the fact that the individual finds himself in the presence of a force which is superior to him and before which he bows; but this force is an entirely natural one. It is not derived from a conventional arrangement which human will has added bodily to natural reality; it issues from innermost reality; it is the necessary product of given causes. Also, recourse to artifice is unnecessary to get the individual to submit to them of his entire free will; it is sufficient to make him become aware of his state of natural dependence and inferiority, whether he forms a tangible and symbolic representation of it through religion or whether he arrives at an adequate and definite notion of it through science. Since the superiority of society to him is not simply physical but intellectual and moral, it has nothing to fear from a critical examination. By making man understand by how much the social being is richer, more complex, and more permanent than the individual being, reflection can only reveal to him the intelligible reasons for the subordination demanded of him and for the sentiments of attachment and respect which habit has fixed in his heart.[24]

It would be only a singularly superficial criticism, therefore, that would attack our concept of social constraint by restating the theories of Hobbes and Machiavelli. But if,

[24] This is why all constraint is not normal and why that constraint which corresponds to some social superiority, i.e., intellectual or moral, alone merits the name. But that which one individual exercises over the other because he is stronger or wealthier, especially if this wealth does not express his social value, is abnormal and can only be maintained by violence.

contrary to these philosophers, we say that social life is natural, our reason is not that we find its source in the nature of the individual. It is natural rather because it springs directly from the collective being which is, itself, a being in its own right, and because it results from special cultivation which individual consciousnesses undergo in their association with each other, an association from which a new form of existence is evolved.[25] If, then, we agree with certain scholars that social reality appears to the individual under the aspect of constraint, we admit with the others that it is a spontaneous product of reality. The tie which binds together these two elements, so contradictory in appearance, is the fact that this reality from which it emanates extends beyond the individual. We mean to say that these words, "constraint" and "spontaneity," have not in our terminology the meaning Hobbes gives to the former and Spencer to the latter.

To summarize, the objection can be raised to most of the attempts which have been made to explain social facts rationally that they have lost sight of all ideas of social discipline or have maintained it only by deceptive subterfuges. The principle we have just expounded would, on the contrary, create a sociology which sees in the spirit of discipline the essential condition of all common life, while at the same time founding it on reason and on truth.

[25] Our theory is even more unlike that of Hobbes than that of natural law. For the partisans of this latter doctrine, collective life is natural only in the measure in which it can be deduced from individual nature. Now, only the most general forms of social organization can, strictly speaking, be derived from this origin. As for the details of social organization, they are too much removed from the extreme indeterminateness of psychological traits to be connected to them; they appear, then, to the disciples of this school quite as artificial as they appear to their adversaries. For us, on the contrary, all is natural, even the most peculiar social order; for all is grounded on the nature of society.

CHAPTER VI

RULES RELATIVE TO ESTABLISHING
SOCIOLOGICAL PROOFS

I

We have only one way to demonstrate that a given phenomenon is the cause of another, viz., to compare the cases in which they are simultaneously present or absent, to see if the variations they present in these different combinations of circumstances indicate that one depends on the other. When they can be artificially produced at the will of the observer, the method is that of experiment, properly so called. When, on the contrary, the production of facts is not within our control and we can only bring them together in the way that they have been spontaneously produced, the method employed is that of indirect experiment, or the comparative method.

We have seen that sociological explanation consists exclusively in establishing relations of causality, that it is a matter of connecting a phenomenon to its cause, or rather a cause to its effects. Since, moreover, social phenomena evidently escape the control of the experimenter, the comparative method is the only one suited to sociology. Comte, it is true, did not judge it sufficient; he found it necessary to complete it by what he called the "historical method," but the reason for this lies in his particular conception of sociological laws.

According to him, they must, above all, reveal not definite relations of causality but the direction which human evolution in general takes; they cannot, then, be discovered by the aid of comparisons, since, to be able to compare the different forms that a social phenomenon takes in different peoples, we must have detached it from the chronological series to which it belongs. If, however, one begins by isolating human development in this way, it becomes impossible to rediscover its sequence. To achieve that aim, we must proceed not by analyses but by broad syntheses. It is necessary to reunite in a single view the successive states of humanity in such a way as to perceive "the continued growth of each human trait, physical, intellectual, moral, and political."[1] Such is the objective of the method that Comte calls "historical" and which, consequently, is stripped of all purpose as soon as one has rejected the fundamental conception of Comtist sociology.

It is true that Mill in his *System of Logic* declares that even indirect experimentation is inapplicable to sociology. But the authority of his argument suffers from the fact that he applied it equally to biological phenomena, and even to the more complex physicochemical phenomena. However, we no longer need to demonstrate today that chemistry and biology can be nothing but experimental sciences; and there is no reason to believe that his criticism is any better founded so far as sociology is concerned, for social phenomena are distinguishable from the former only by a greater complexity. This difference may perhaps imply that the use of experimental reasoning offers more difficulties in sociology than in the other sciences, but it does not follow that it would be absolutely impossible.

This entire theory of Mill's rests on a postulate which is, no doubt, tied up with the fundamental principles of his logic but which contradicts all the results of science. He ad-

[1] *Cours de philosophie positive*, IV, 328.

mits, in fact, that the same consequence does not always result from the same antecedent but may be due now to one cause, now to another. This conception of the causal bond, by removing all determinism from it, makes it almost inaccessible to scientific analysis, for it introduces such complications in the entanglement of causes and effects that the mind is irretrievably lost in them. If it is true that an effect can follow from different causes, then, in order to learn what determines a given result in a given set of circumstances, it would be necessary to conduct the experiment in an isolation practically unrealizable in sociology.

This supposed axiom of the plurality of causes is, in fact, a negation of the principle of causality. To be sure, if one believes with Mill that cause and effect are absolutely unrelated, there is nothing contradictory in admitting that an effect may follow sometimes one cause and sometimes another. If the relation which unites C to A is purely chronological, it does not exclude another relation of the same kind which would unite, for example, C to B.

If, on the contrary, the causal bond is something logical, it could not be indeterminate. If it consists in a relation resulting from the nature of things, a given effect can maintain this relationship with only one cause, for it can express only one single nature. However, only philosophers have ever questioned the logic of the causal relation. For the scientist there is no question about it; it is assumed by the very method of science. How could one explain otherwise both the very important role of deduction in experimental reasoning and the fundamental principle of proportionality between cause and effect? In order that the cases in which one claims to observe a plurality of causes may be decisive, it would be necessary to have established beforehand either that this plurality is not simply apparent or that the supposed unity of the effect does not proceed from real plurality of causes. Many times it has happened that science has reduced to unity causes whose diversity, at first sight, seemed irreducible. John Stuart Mill, himself, gives an example of it when he recalls that, according to modern theories, the production of heat by friction, percussion, chemical action, etc., is in reality only a product from the same single cause. Conversely, when it is a question of effect, the scientist often distinguishes where the layman confuses. For common sense, the word "fever" designates one single morbid condition; for science, there are many fevers, specifically different, and the causes are as numerous as are the effects; and if, among all these pathological types, there is nevertheless something in common, it is because these causes, similarly, have certain characteristics in common.

It is all the more important to cast out this principle from sociology since a number of sociologists still feel the influence of it, even though they do not object to the use of the comparative method. Thus, it is commonly said that crime may be produced by several different causes and that the same is true with suicide, punishment, etc. If we practice experimental reasoning in this spirit, we shall assemble in vain a considerable number of facts, for we shall never be able to obtain precise laws or determinate relations of causality. We shall be able only to assign vaguely a badly defined consequence to a confused and indefinite group of antecedents. If, then, we wish to employ the comparative method in a scientific manner, i.e., by conforming to the principle of causality as it occurs in science itself, we shall have to take as the basis of our comparisons the following proposition: *A given effect has always a single corresponding cause.* Thus, returning to the examples cited above, if suicide depends on more than one cause, it is because, in reality, there are several kinds of suicides. The same is true of crime. For punishment, on the contrary, if it has seemed possible to explain it equally well by different causes, the reason is that we have not yet been able to perceive the common element in all these antecedents, by virtue of which they produce their common effect.[2]

II

Nevertheless, if all the diverse procedures of the comparative method are proved to be applicable to sociology, it does not follow that they are all of equal validity. The so-called method of "residues"—if, indeed, it does constitute a form of experimental reasoning—is of no particular use in the study of social phenomena. Apart from the fact that it can be useful only in the rather advanced sciences, since it supposes an important number of laws to exist already, social phenomena are much too complex for the effect of all the causes, excepting one, to be removed in a given case.

The use of the methods both of agreement and difference is difficult for the same reason. They suppose that the causes compared either agree or differ by one single point. In all probability, no science has ever been able to perform experiments in which the truly unique character of an agreement or a difference was irrefutably established. Some alternative antecedent which varies directly with the single known antecedent may have escaped one's notice. The absolute elimination of adventitious elements is an ideal which cannot really be attained; nevertheless the physicochemical and even the biological sciences approach it closely enough, in a

[2] *Division du travail social*, p. 87.

great number of cases, so that the demonstration can be regarded as practically sufficient. But the situation is not the same in sociology, owing to the too great complexity of the phenomena and the impossibility of all artificial experiments. As an even approximately complete inventory could not be made of all the facts which coexist within a given society or which have succeeded one another in the course of its history, one can never be even approximately certain that two societies agree or differ in all respects save one. The chances of allowing a phenomenon to escape are far greater than those of observing all. Consequently, such a method of demonstration can yield only conjectures which, when considered by themselves, are almost devoid of all scientific value.

But the case is quite different with the method of concomitant variations or correlation. For this method to be reliable, it is not necessary that all the variables differing from those which we are comparing shall have been strictly excluded. The mere parallelism of the series of values presented by the two phenomena, provided that it has been established in a sufficient number and variety of cases, is proof that a relationship exists between them. Its validity is due to the fact that the concomitant variations display the causal relationship not by coincidençe, as the preceding ones do, but intrinsically. It does not simply show us two facts which accompany or exclude one another externally,[3] so that there is no direct proof that they are united by an internal bond; on the contrary, it shows them as mutually influencing each other in a continuous manner, at least so far as their

[3] In the case of the method of difference, the absence of the cause excludes the presence of the effect.

quality is concerned. This interaction, in itself, suffices to demonstrate that they are not foreign to each other.

The manner in which a phenomenon develops, expresses its nature. For two developments to correspond to each other, there must also be a correspondence in the natures manifested by them. Constant concomitance is, then, a law in itself, whatever may be the condition of the phenomena excluded from the comparison. Thus, to invalidate the proof, it is not sufficient to show that it is contradicted by a few particular applications of the method of agreement or difference. That would be to attribute to this kind of proof an authority which it cannot have in sociology. When two phenomena vary directly with each other, this relationship must be accepted even when, in certain cases, one of these phenomena should be present without the other. For it may be either that the cause has been prevented from producing its effect by the action of some contrary cause or that it is present but in a form different from the one previously observed. No doubt, we need, as we say, to examine the facts anew; but certainly we must not abandon hastily the results of a methodically conducted demonstration.

It is true that the laws established by this procedure are not always presented at the outset in the form of relations of causality. The concomitance may be due not to the fact that one phenomenon is the cause of the other but to the fact that they are both the effects of the same cause, or, again, that there exists between them a third phenomenon, interposed but unperceived, which is the effect of the first and the cause of the second. The results to which this method leads need, therefore, to be interpreted. But what experimental method is there which obtains mechanically a relation of causality without some analysis of the observed data? It is essential only that this elaboration be methodically conducted, and here we shall proceed as follows.

We shall first investigate, by the aid of deduction, how one of the two terms has produced the other; then we shall try to verify the result of this deduction with the aid of experiments, i.e., new comparisons. If the deduction is possible and if the verification succeeds, we can regard the proof as completed. If, on the contrary, we are aware of no direct bond between these facts, especially if the hypothesis of such a bond contradicts laws already demonstrated, we shall begin to look for a third phenomenon on which the other two depend equally or which have served as an intermediary between them.

For example, we can establish in the most certain way that the tendency to suicide varies directly with education. But it is impossible to understand how erudition can lead to suicide; such an explanation is in contradiction to the laws of psychology. Education, especially the elementary branches of knowledge, reaches only the more superficial regions of consciousness; the instinct of self-preservation is, on the contrary, one of our fundamental tendencies. It could not, then, be appreciably affected by a phenomenon as far removed and of so feeble an influence. Thus we come to ask if both facts are not the consequence of an identical condition. This common cause is the weakening of religious traditionalism, which reinforces both the need for knowledge and the tendency toward suicide.

But there is another reason which makes the method of concomitant variations the instrument par excellence of sociological research. Even when circumstances are most favorable to them, the other methods can be employed successfully only if the number of facts compared is very considerable. If one cannot find two societies which differ from, or resemble, one another in only one point, one must at least be able to establish that, in general, two facts either accompany or exclude each other. But, in order that this discovery may have scientific value, it must have been made a very great number of times; one would almost need to be assured that all the facts have been reviewed. Not only is an inventory as complete as this impossible, but also the facts thus accumulated can never be established with sufficient precision, because they are too numerous. Not only does one risk omitting some of the essential facts which contradict those which are known, but one is not sure of knowing the latter well. In fact, the conclusions of sociologists have often been discredited because they have chosen the method of agreement or of difference—especially the former—and have occupied themselves more with accumulating documents than with selecting and criticizing them. Thus it often happens that they assign the same value to the confused, hastily made observations of travelers as to the carefully prepared texts of history. When we see these demonstrations, not only can we not avoid saying to ourselves that a single fact could invalidate them but the very facts on which they are established do not always inspire confidence.

The method of concomitant variations compels us to accept neither these incomplete enumerations nor these superficial observations. In order to obtain results, a few facts suffice. As soon as one has proved that, in a certain number of cases, two phenomena vary with one another, one is certain of being in the presence of a law. Having no need to be numerous, the documents can be selected and, further, studied more closely by the sociologist. He will then be able to take as the principal material for his inductions the societies whose beliefs, traditions, customs, and law have taken shape in written and authentic documents. To be sure, he will not spurn the information offered by uncritical ethnography (there are no facts which may be disdained by the scientist), but he will put them in their true place. Instead of making this the center of gravity of his researches, he will in general utilize it only as a supplement to historical data; or, at the very least, he will try to confirm it by the latter. Not only will he thus limit more intelligently the extent of his comparisons, but he will conduct them with a more critical spirit; for, by the very fact that he will confine himself to a restricted order of facts, he will be able to check them with more care. No doubt, he does not need again to work over the research of historians, but neither can he welcome passively and naïvely every bit of information which comes to his hand.

But we must not believe that sociology is substantially inferior to the other sciences merely because it can use only a single experimental method. This inconvenience is, indeed, compensated by the wealth of variations at the disposal of the sociologist, of which we find no example in the other realms of nature. The changes which take place in an organism in the course of an individual existence are few in number and very restricted; those that one can produce artificially without destroying life are themselves narrowly limited. It is true that more important changes have been produced in the course of zoölogical evolution; but there are left only rare and obscure vestiges of these, and it is difficult to rediscover the conditions which determined them.

Social life, on the contrary, is an uninterrupted series of transformations, parallel to other transformations in the conditions of collective existence; and we have at our disposal data concerning not only the transformations of recent epochs but many of those through which extinct peoples have passed. In spite of its gaps, the history of humanity is clear and complete in a different way from that of animal species. Furthermore, a large number of social phenomena exist which occur throughout the entire extent of society but which take on diverse forms according to geographical location, profession, religous faiths, etc. Such are, for example, crime, suicide, birth-rate, marriage-rates, practice of thrift, etc. From the diversity of these special milieus will result, for each of these orders of facts, new series of variations, outside those which historic evolution produces. If, then, the sociologist cannot employ with equal efficacy all the procedures of experimental research, the single method which he must use, almost to the exclusion of the others, can be very fertile in his hands, because of his incomparable resources for applying it.

Unless it is applied with care and precision, however, it does not produce its best results. One proves nothing when, as so often happens, one is content to show by more or less numerous examples that, in scattered cases, the facts have varied as the hypothesis demands. From these sporadic and fragmentary agreements one can draw no general conclusion. To illustrate the idea is not to demonstrate it. It is necessary to compare not isolated variations but a series of systematically arranged variations of wide range, in which the individual items tie up with one another in as continuous a gradation as possible. For the variations of a phenomenon permit inductive generalizations only if they reveal clearly the manner in which they develop under given circumstances. There must be between them the same sequence as between the different stages of a given natural evolution; and, in addition, the evolutionary trend that they establish ought to be sufficiently extended as to lend some certainty to its direction.

III

But the way in which these series must be formed differs according to the case. They can include facts borrowed either from a single and unique society, from several societies of the same species, or from several distinct social species.

The first process may suffice, if absolutely necessary, when it is a matter of facts that are widely distributed and on which we have statistical information that is rather extensive and varied. For example, when comparing the curve which expresses the trend of suicide during a sufficiently long period of time with the variations which the same phenomenon presents according to provinces, classes, rural or urban areas, sex, age, social status, etc., one can arrive, even without extending one's researches beyond a single country, at establishing genuine laws, although it is always preferable to confirm these results by other observations made on other peoples of the same species. But one can only be content with comparisons as limited as these when one studies one of the social currents extending throughout the entire society. When, on the contrary, it is a matter of an institution, a legal or moral regulation, or an established custom which functions in the same manner over the entire extent of the country and which changes only in time, one cannot limit one's self to the study of a single people. In this case, the data would comprise only a single pair of parallel curves, namely, the curve which shows the progression in history of the phenomenon considered and the curve of the supposed cause in this single society. Of course, even this single parallelism, if constant, is already a fact of considerable importance; but it could not, in itself, constitute a demonstration.

By including in the computation several peoples of the same species, we have at our disposal a more extended field of comparison. First of all, we can compare the history of one with that of the others and observe whether or not in each one of them, taken by itself, the same phenomenon evolves in time as a result of the same conditions. Then one can establish comparisons between these various developments. For example, one will determine the form that the fact under consideration assumes in these different societies at its highest development. Since these forms are distinct individualities while belonging to the same type, this form is not everywhere the same; it is more or less distinct according to the particular case. One will thus have a new series of variations with which to compare the forms which appear at the corresponding stage in each one of these societies. Thus, after having followed the evolution of the patriarchal family through the history of Rome, Athens, and Sparta, we shall classify these same city-states according to the maximum degree of development that this family type attains in each of them; and we shall then see whether they are still to be classified in the same way as in the first experiment, when they were ranked in accordance with the social milieu, which presumably conditioned that type.

But this method in itself can scarcely be sufficient. It applies, in fact, only to phenomena which originated during the life of the peoples compared. A society, however, does not create its organization entirely alone; it receives it, in part, ready-made from preceding societies. What is thus transmitted to it is not the product of any development in the course of its history, and consequently cannot be explained unless one transgresses the boundaries of the species in question. Only the growth which is added to this original culture base and which transforms the borrowed element can be treated in this narrower manner. But the higher the social scale, the less important are the characteristics developed by each people, as compared to its borrowed culture traits. Such is, of course, the condition of all progress.

Thus, the new elements that we have introduced into domestic law, property law, and morality, since the beginning of our history, are relatively few and unimportant, compared with those which the past has bequeathed to us. Therefore, the changes and innovations which occur cannot be understood if one does not first study these more fundamental phenomena which are their roots; and they can only be studied by the aid of much more extended comparisons. To be able to explain the present state of the family, marriage, property, etc., it would be necessary to know their origins and the elements of which these institutions are composed. On these points the comparative history of the great European societies could not give us much light. We must go farther back.

Consequently, to explain a social institution belonging to a given species, one will compare its different forms, not only among peoples of that species but in all preceding species as well. For example, in the matter of domestic organization the most rudimentary type that has ever existed will first be established, in order that the manner in which it grew progressively more complex may then be followed, step by step. This method, which may be called "genetic," would give at once the analysis and the synthesis of the phenomenon. For, on the one hand, it would show us the separate elements composing it, by the very fact that it would allow us to see the process of accretion or action. At the same time, thanks to this wide field of comparison, we should be in a much better position to determine the conditions on which depend their formation. *Consequently, one cannot explain a social fact of any complexity except by following its complete development through all social species.* Comparative sociology is not a particular branch of sociology; it is sociology itself, in so far as it ceases to be purely descriptive and aspires to account for facts.

In the course of these extended comparisons, an error is often committed with correspondingly misleading results. At times, in order to judge the direction in which social events develop, it has happened that scholars have simply compared what occurs at the decline of each species with what happens at the beginning of the succeeding species. Proceeding thus, it has been said, for example, that the weakening of religious beliefs and all traditionalism could never be anything but a transitory phenomenon in the life of peoples, because it appears only during the last period of their existence and ceases as soon as a new stage begins. But, with such a method, one is tempted to take as the regular and necessary march of progress that which was simply the effect of an entirely different cause. In fact, any certain stage of a young society is not simply the prolongation of the stage of the preceding declining society. On the contrary, it is conditioned in part by the very fact of its youth, which prevents the products of the knowledge acquired by former peoples from being immediately assimilated and utilized. Thus the child receives from his parents faculties and predispositions which come into play in his life only belatedly. It is therefore possible that the return to traditionalism observed at the beginning of the history of each individual society is due not to the fact that an eclipse of the phenomenon can be only transitory but to the special conditions in which every young society is placed. The comparison can be valid only if we remove this disturbing factor of age. To arrive at a just comparison, *it will suffice to consider the societies compared at the same period of their development.* Thus, in order to know in what direction a social phenomenon is evolving, one will compare the youth of each species with the youth of the succeeding species, and, according as (from one of these stages to the next) it presents more, less, or equal complexity, one can say that it progresses, retrogresses, or maintains itself.

CONCLUSION

To sum up, the distinctive characteristics of our method are as follows: First, it is entirely independent of philosophy. Because sociology had its birth in the great philosophical doctrines, it has retained the habit of relying on some philosophical system and thus has been continuously overburdened with it. It has been successively positivistic, evolutionary, idealistic, when it should have been content to be simply sociology. We should even hesitate to describe it as naturalistic, unless the term indicates merely that the sociologist considers social facts as capable of being explained naturally, or that he is a scientist and not a mystic. We reject the term if it is given a doctrinal meaning concerning the essence of social objects—if, e.g., by it is meant that social objects are reducible to the other cosmic forces.

Sociology does not need to choose between the great hypotheses which divide metaphysicians. It needs to embrace free will no more than determinism. All that it asks is that the principle of causality be applied to social phenomena. Again, this principle is enunciated for sociology not as a rational necessity but only as an empirical postulate, produced by legitimate induction. Since the law of causality has been verified in the other realms of nature, and since it has progressively extended its authority from the physicochemical world to the biological, and from the latter to the psychological, we are justified in claiming that it is equally true of the social world; and it is possible to add today that the researches undertaken on the basis of this postulate tend to confirm it. However, the question as to whether the nature of the causal bond excludes all chance is not thereby settled.

This emancipation of sociology is decidedly to the advantage of philosophy. For, in so far as the sociologist has not sufficiently eliminated philosophy from social science, he considers social facts only from their most general aspect, the aspect from which they most resemble the other things in the universe. Now, if sociology, thus conceived, serves to illustrate philosophy with curious facts, it does not enrich it with new views, since it points out nothing new in the objects which it studies. But, if the fundamental facts of the other fields of knowledge actually recur in the social field, they do so under special forms, which clarify the nature of these facts since they are their highest expression. However, in order to treat them from this aspect, we must leave generalities behind and enter into the detail of facts. Thus, as sociology becomes specialized, it will furnish more original materials for philosophical reflection.

All this has already given us an idea of how the essential concepts, such as those of species, organ, function, health and morbidity, cause and effect, appear in sociology under entirely new aspects. Moreover, may not sociology feature an idea which might well be the basis not only of a psychology but of a whole philosophy—the idea of association?

With reference to practical social doctrines, our method permits and commands the same independence. Sociology thus understood will be neither individualistic, communistic, nor socialistic in the sense commonly given these words. On principle, it will ignore these theories, in which it could not recognize any scientific value, since they tend not to describe or interpret, but to reform, social organization. At least, if it takes an interest in them, it is in proportion as it sees in them social facts which can aid it both in understanding the social reality and in disclosing the needs that are the motivating power in society. We do not mean, however, that it ought to take no interest in practical questions. It has been evident, on the contrary, that our constant preoccupation has been to orient it so that it might have practical results. It necessarily meets these problems at the end of its researches. But, by the very fact that they present themselves to sociology only at this moment, and that, consequently, they are derived from facts and not from emotions, one can foresee that they must be formulated for the sociologist in quite other terms than for the masses, and that the tentative solutions it can give them could not coincide exactly with any of those which now satisfy various interest groups. But the role of sociology from this point of view must properly consist in emancipating us from all parties, not to the extent of negating all doctrine, but by persuading us to assume toward these questions a special attitude that science alone can give in its direct contact with things. Science alone can teach us to treat historic institutions, whatever they may be, with respect but without mystic awe, by making us appreciate both their permanent and their ephemeral aspects, their stability and their infinite variability.

In the second place, our method is objective. It is dominated entirely by the idea that social facts are things and must be treated as such. No doubt, this principle is found again, under a slightly different form, at the basis of the doctrines of Comte and Spencer. But these great thinkers gave it theoretic formulation without putting it into practice. In order that it might not remain a dead letter, it is not sufficient to promulgate it; it is necessary to make it the basis of an entire discipline which will take hold of the student at the very moment he approaches the subject of his researches, and which will accompany him, step by step, in all his proceedings. We have devoted ourselves to instituting this discipline.

We have shown how the sociologist has to disregard the preconceptions which he had of facts, in order to face the facts themselves; how he has to discriminate among them according to their most objective characteristics; how he must seek in the facts themselves the means of classifying them as normal and pathological; how, finally, he must be inspired by the same principle in the explanations he attempts as in the way in which he tests these explanations. For, as soon as he has the feeling that he is in the presence of things, he will no longer think of explaining them by utilitarian calculations or by syllogistic reasonings of any sort. He will understand too well the gap that exists between such causes and such effects.

A thing is a force which can be engendered only by another force. In rendering an account of social facts, we seek, then, energies capable of producing them. Not only do the explanations thus given differ from the preceding ones, but they are differently verified, or, rather, it is only with them that the need of verification is felt. If sociological phenomena are only systems of objectivized ideas, to explain them is to rethink them in their logical order, and this explanation is in itself its own proof; at the very most, it will require confirmation by a few examples. Only methodical experiments, on the contrary, can extract from things their real secrets.

If we consider social facts as things, we consider them as *social things*. The third trait that characterizes our method is that it is exclusively sociological. It has often appeared that these phenomena, because of their extreme complexity, were either inhospitable to science or could be subject to it only when reduced to their elemental conditions, either psychic or organic, that is, only when stripped of their proper nature. We have, on the contrary, undertaken to establish that it is possible to treat them scientifically without removing any of their distinctive characteristics. We have even refused to identify the immateriality which characterizes them with the complex immateriality of psychological phenomena; we have, furthermore, refused to reabsorb it, with the Italian school, into the general properties of organized matter.[1] We have shown that a social fact can be explained only by another social fact; and, at the same time, we have shown how this sort of explanation is possible by pointing out, in the internal social milieu, the principal factor in collective evolution. Sociology is, then, not an auxiliary of any other science; it is itself a distinct and autonomous science, and the feeling of the specificity of social reality is indeed so necessary to the sociologist that only distinctly sociological training can prepare him to grasp social facts intelligently.

In our opinion this progress is the most important that sociology still has to make. No doubt, when a science is in the process of being born, one is obliged, in order to construct it, to refer to the only models that exist, namely, the sciences already formed. These contain a treasure of experiences which it would be foolish to ignore. A science can regard itself as definitely established, however, only when it has achieved independence for itself. For it can justify its existence only when it has for its subject matter an order of

[1] Our method has, therefore, been quite wrongly described as "materialistic."

facts which the other sciences do not study. It is impossible that the same concepts can fit equally well things of different natures.

Such appear to us to be the principles of sociological method. This collection of rules will perhaps appear needlessly complicated if one compares it with the procedures in current use. All this apparatus of precautions may seem very laborious for a science which, up to this point, scarcely demanded from those who devoted themselves to it more than general and philosophical training. It is certain, indeed, that the practice of such a method cannot have for its effect the popularization of interest in sociological matters. When, as a condition of their acceptance into the sociological fraternity, we ask men to discard the concepts they are accustomed to apply to an order of facts, in order to re-examine the latter in a new way, we cannot expect to recruit a numerous clientele. But this is not the goal toward which we are heading. We believe, on the contrary, that the time has come for sociology to spurn popular success, so to speak, and to assume the exacting character befitting every science. It will then gain in dignity and authority what it will perhaps lose in popularity. For, so long as it remains involved in partisan struggles, is content to expound common ideas with more logic than the layman, and, consequently, presumes no special competence, it has no right to speak loudly enough to silence passions and prejudices. Assuredly, the time when it will be able to play this role successfully is still far off. However, we must begin to work now, in order to put it in condition to fill this role some day.